La vita sotto il mare Oceano
Bambini Libro da colorare

Young Scholar

**All rights reserved. No part of this document may be reproduced
Used or transmitted in any form or by any means, electronic or otherwise. This means you
cannot photocopy any material ideas or tips that are provided in this book.**

Young Scholar
An imprint of Ciparum LLC

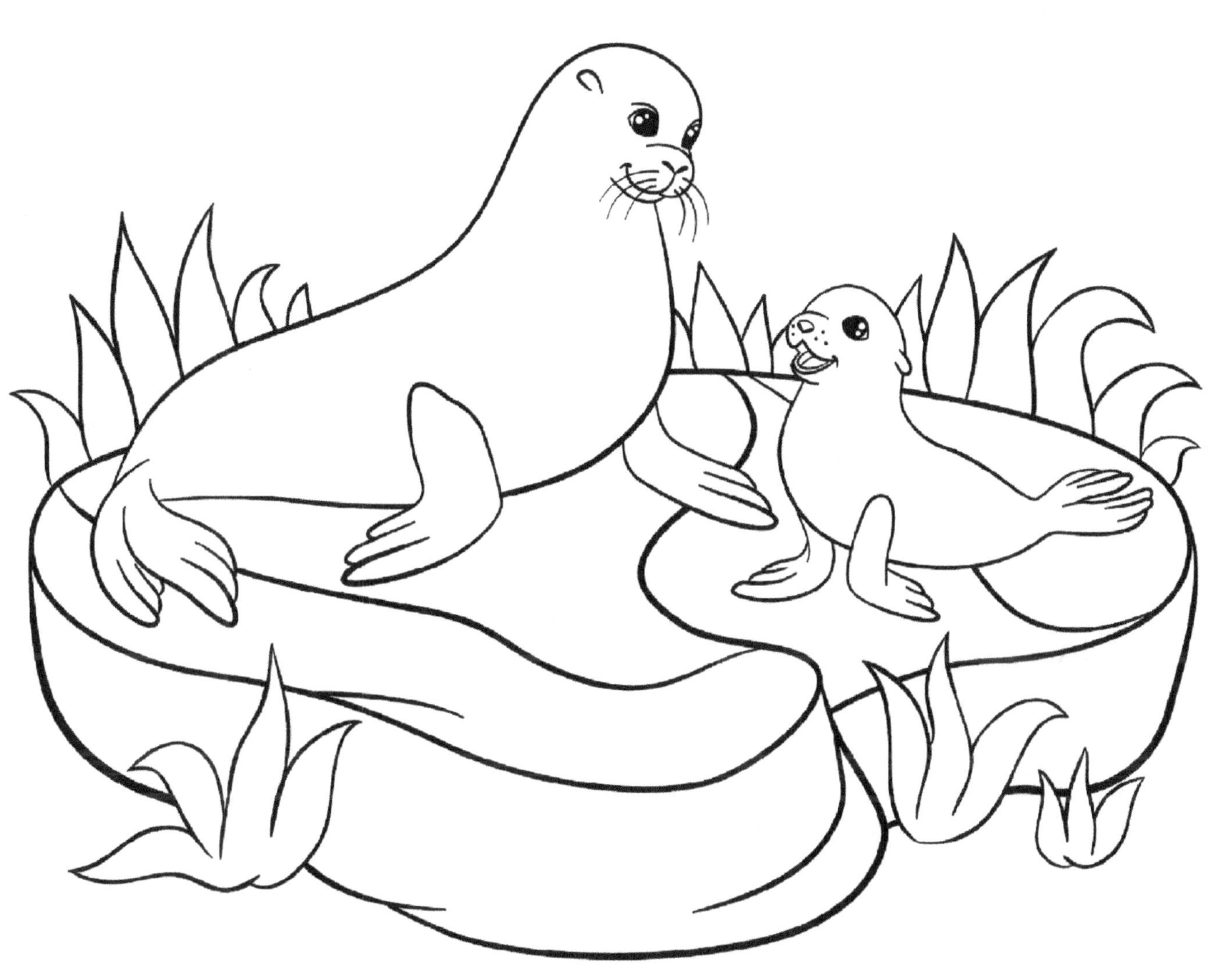

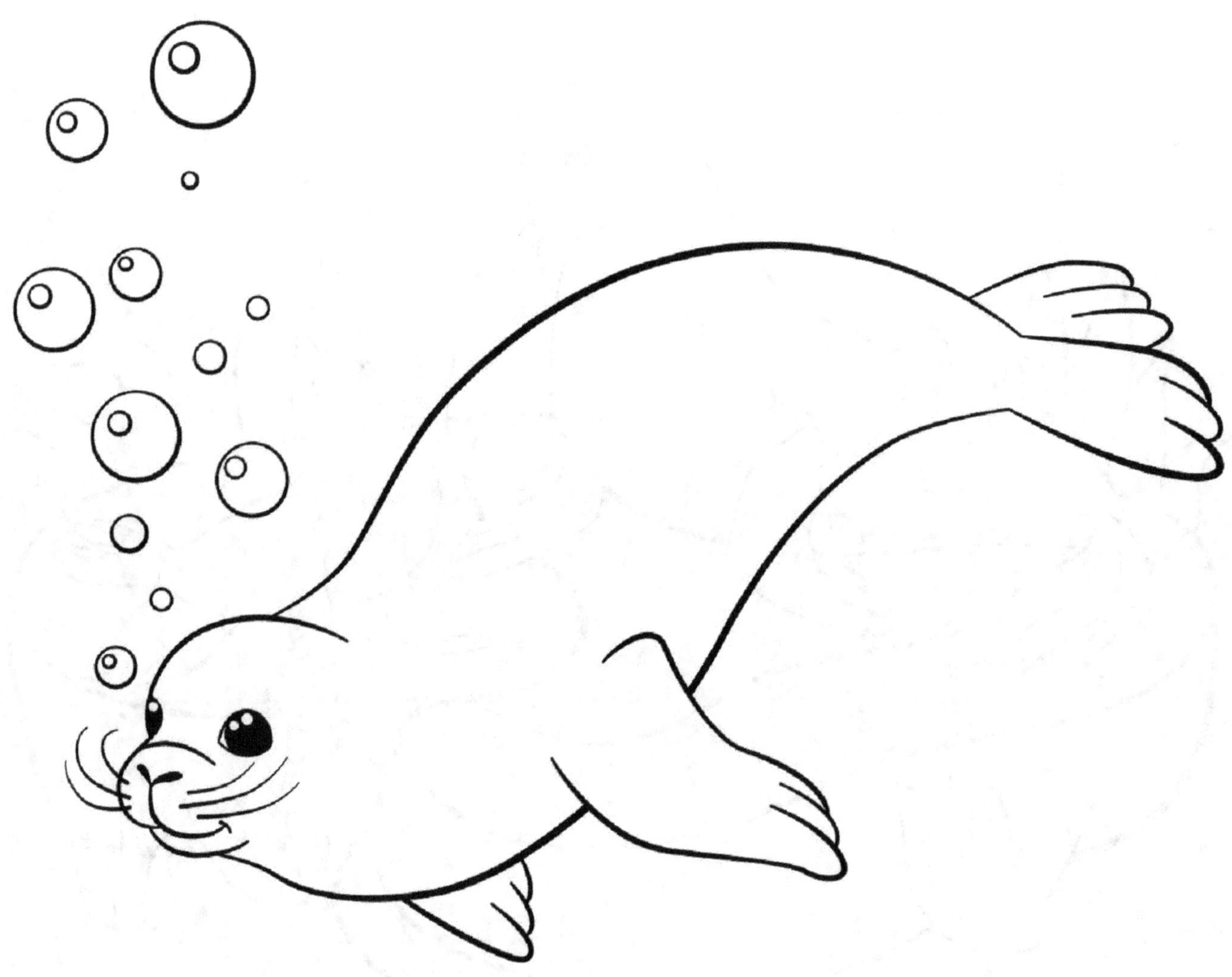

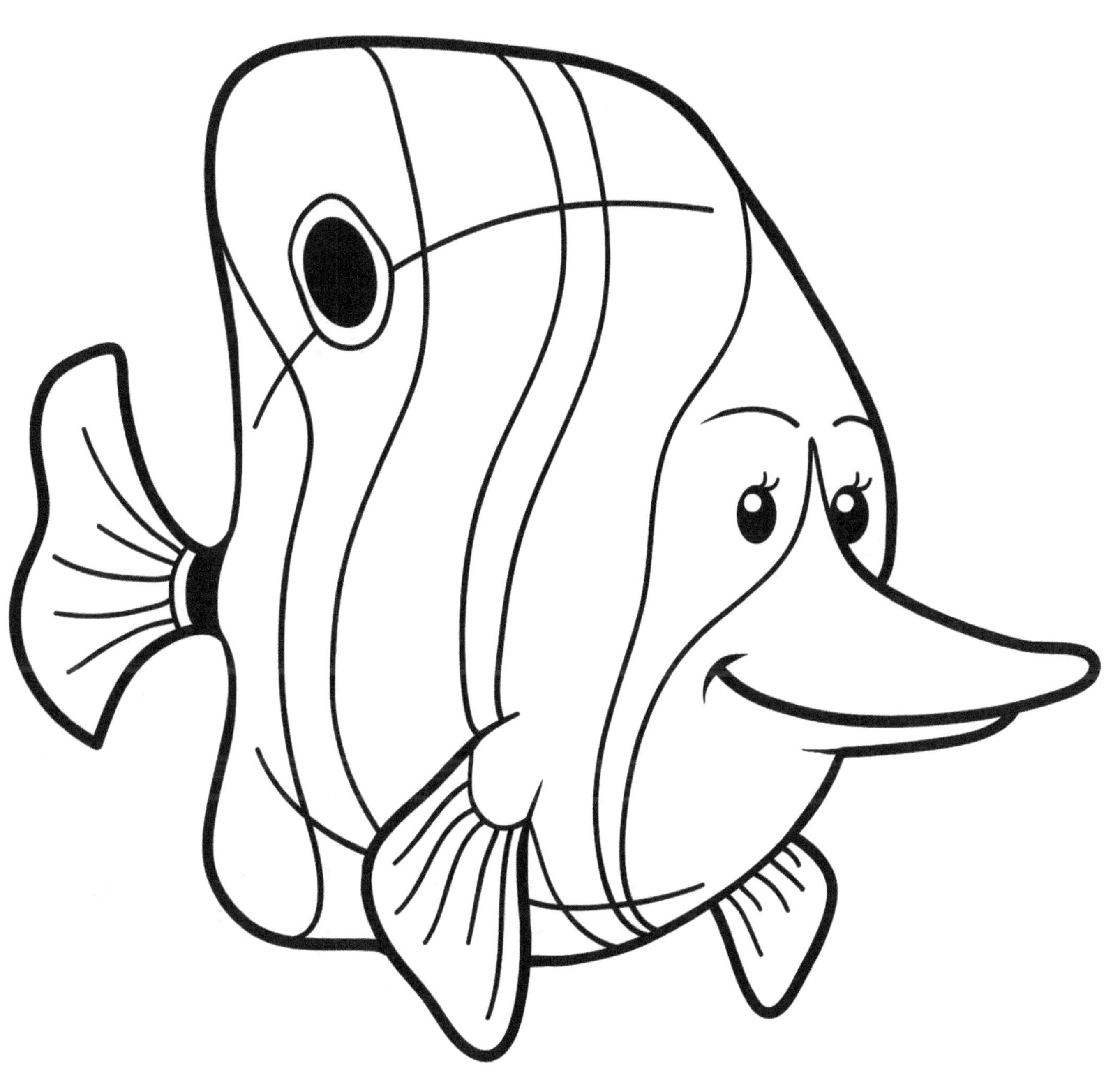

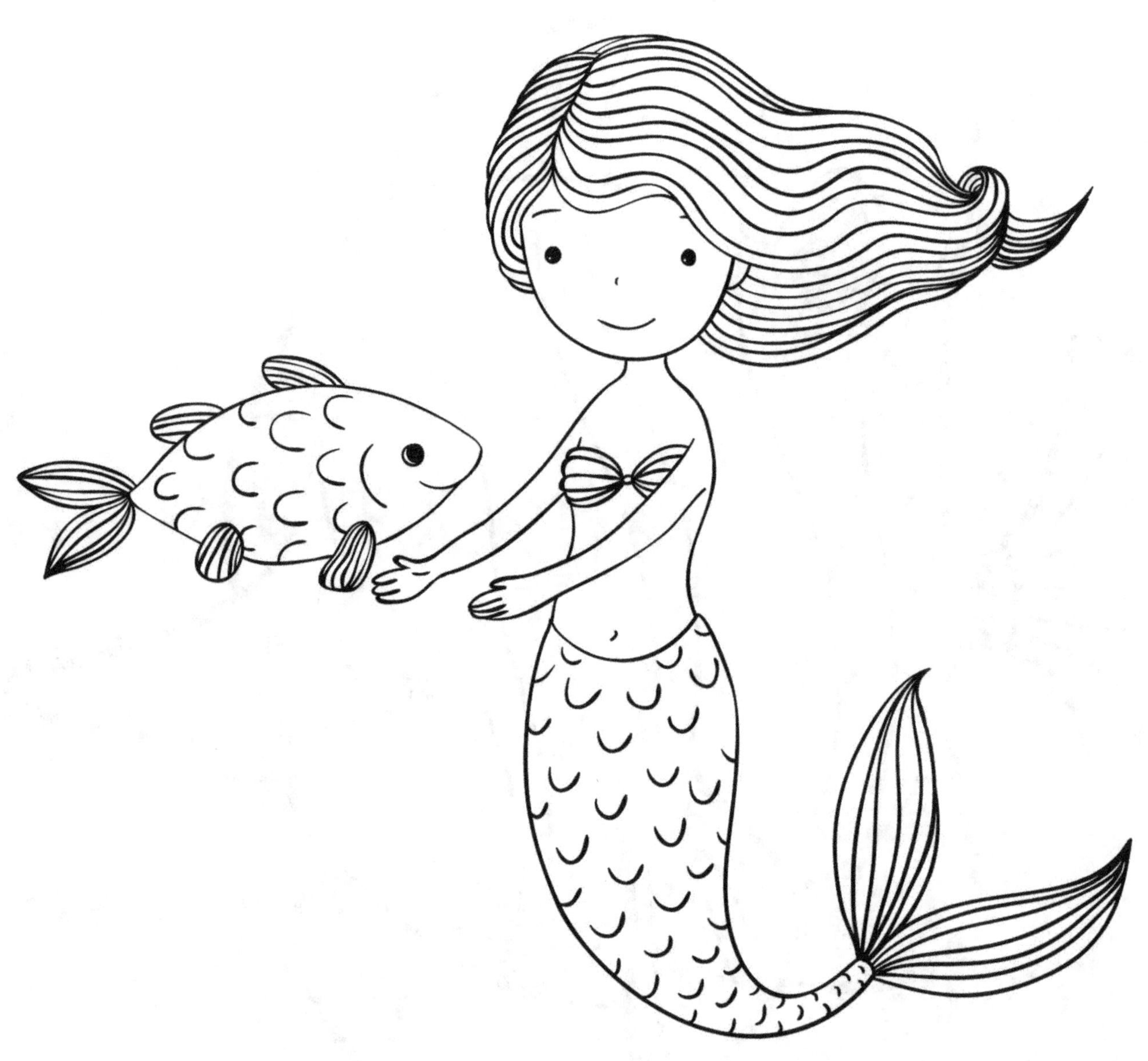

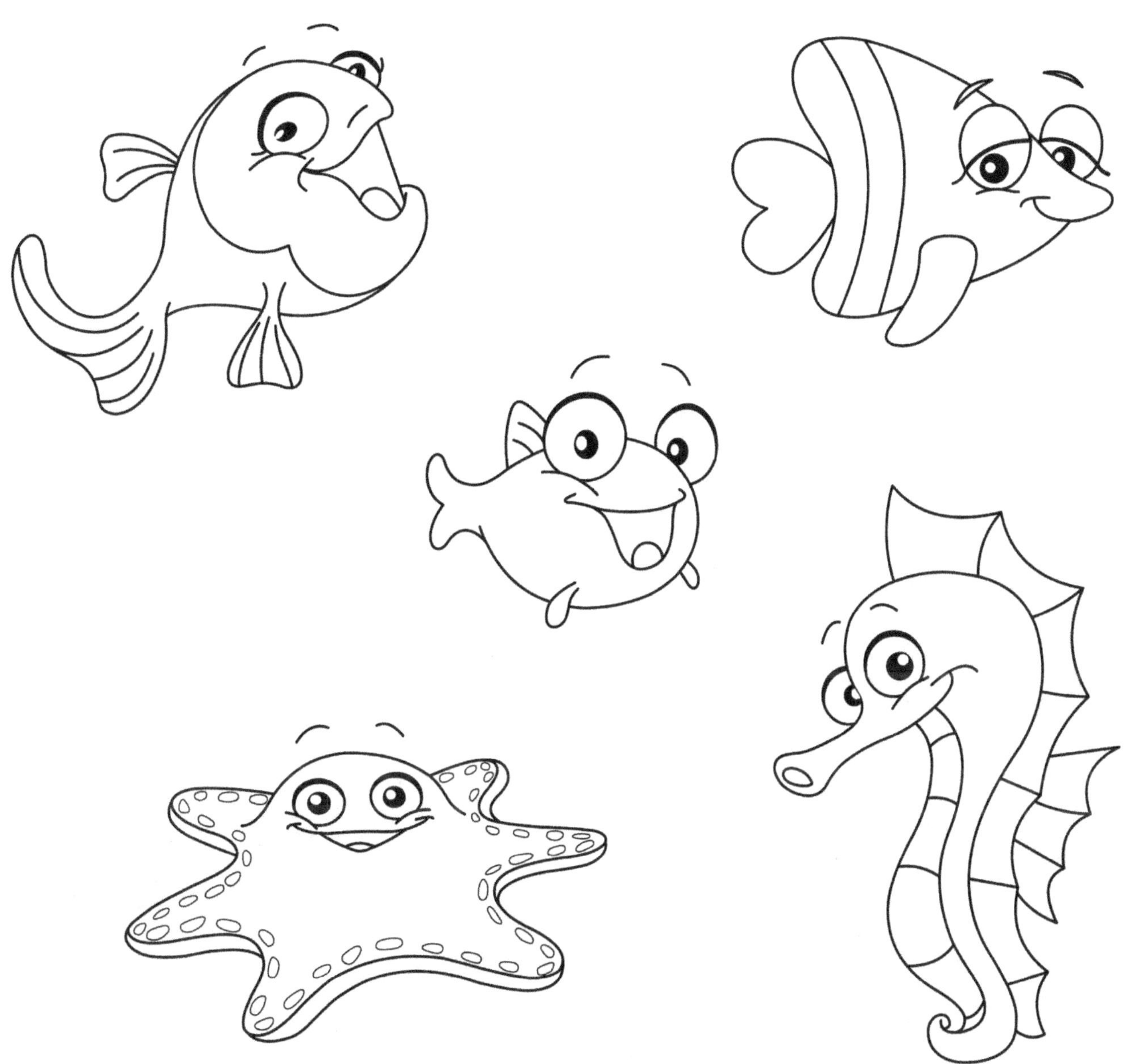

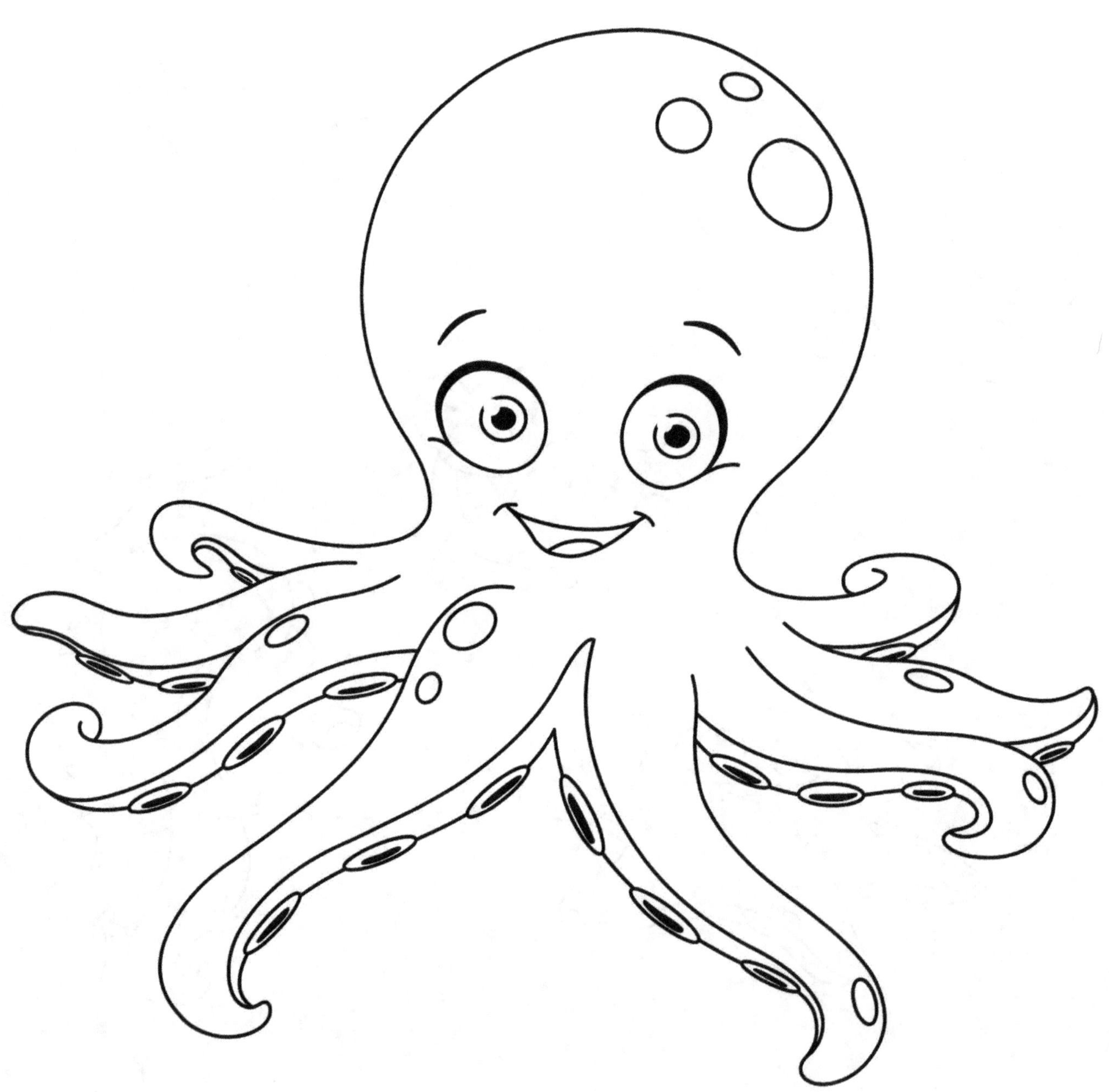

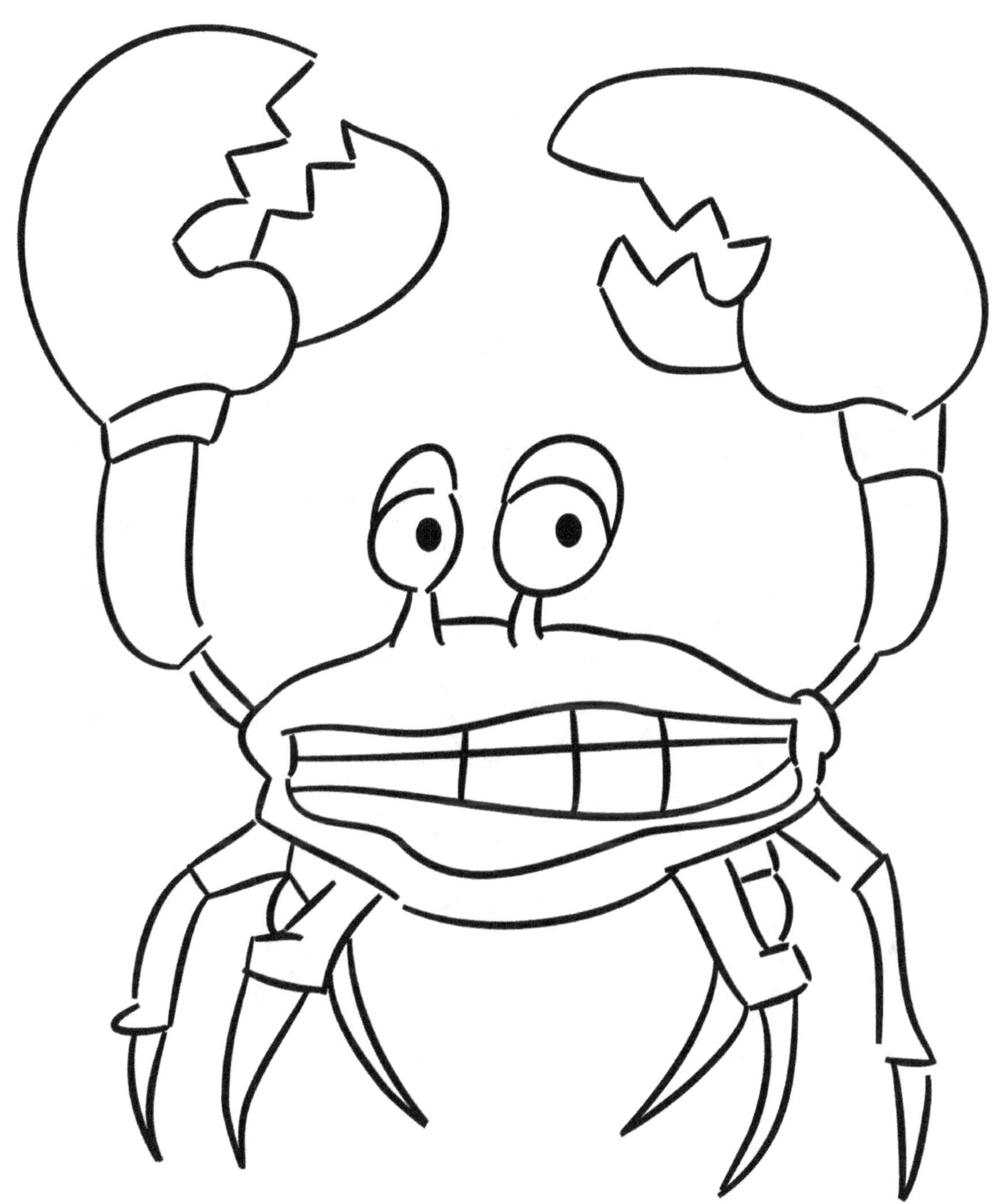

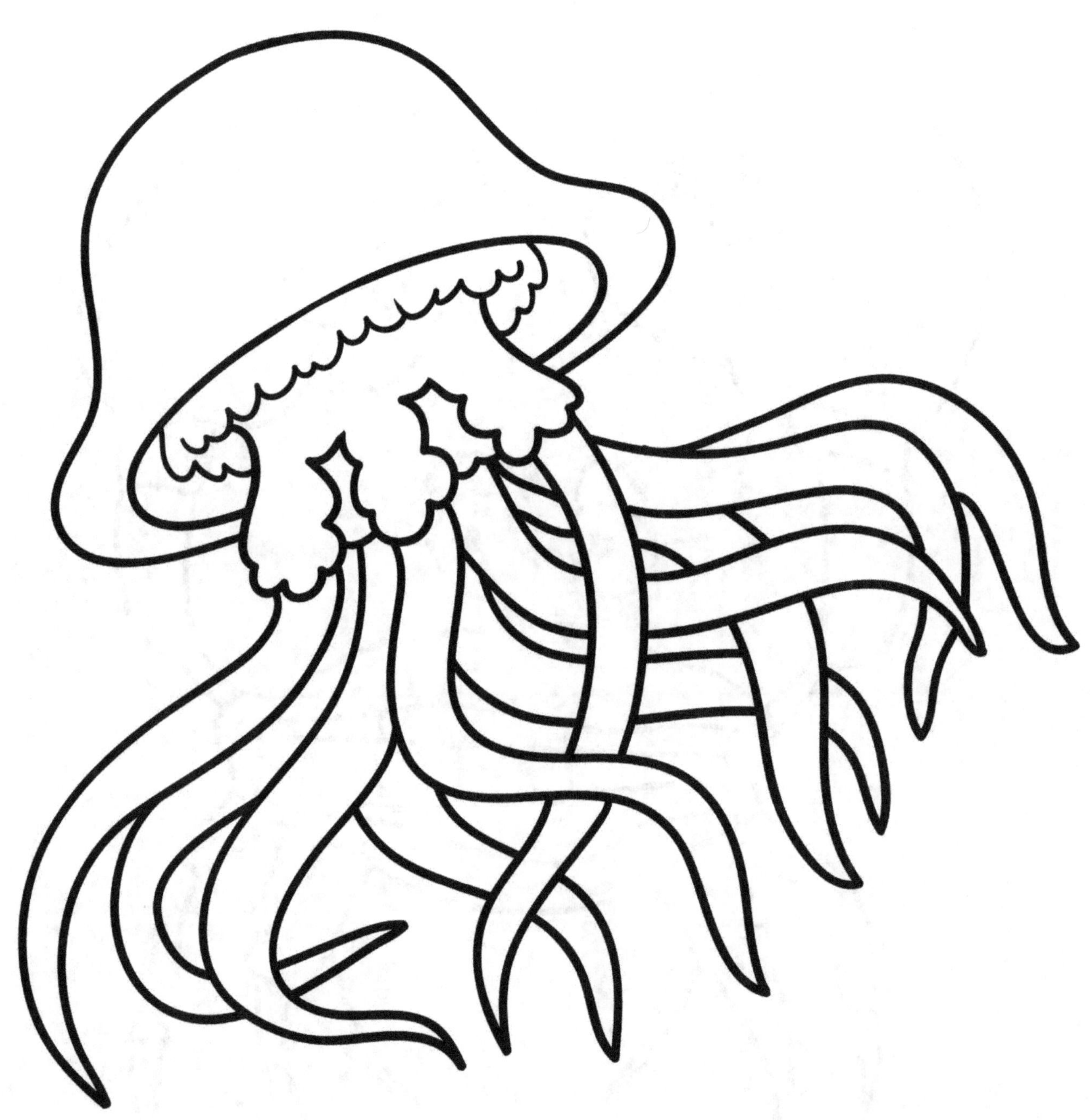

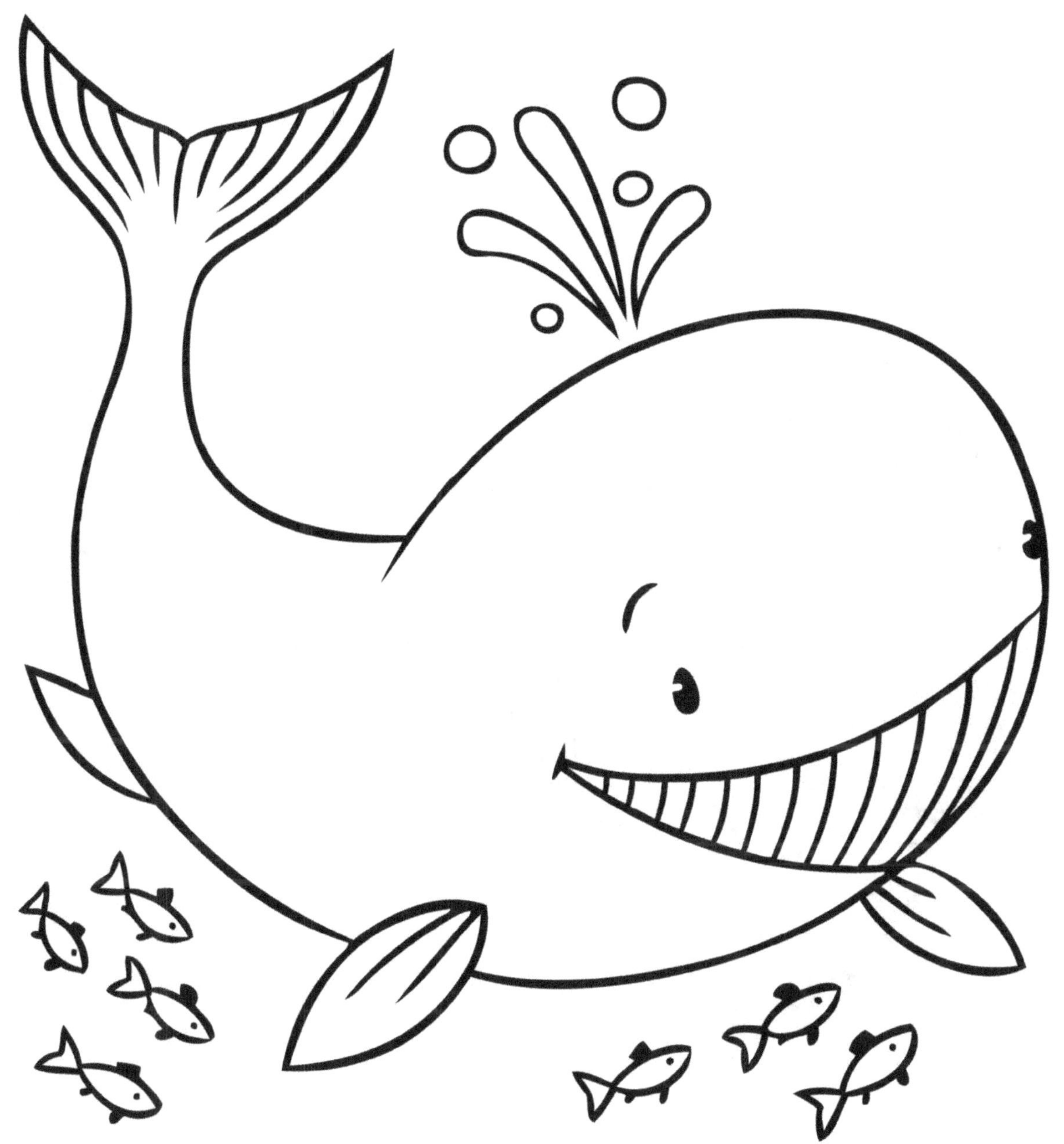

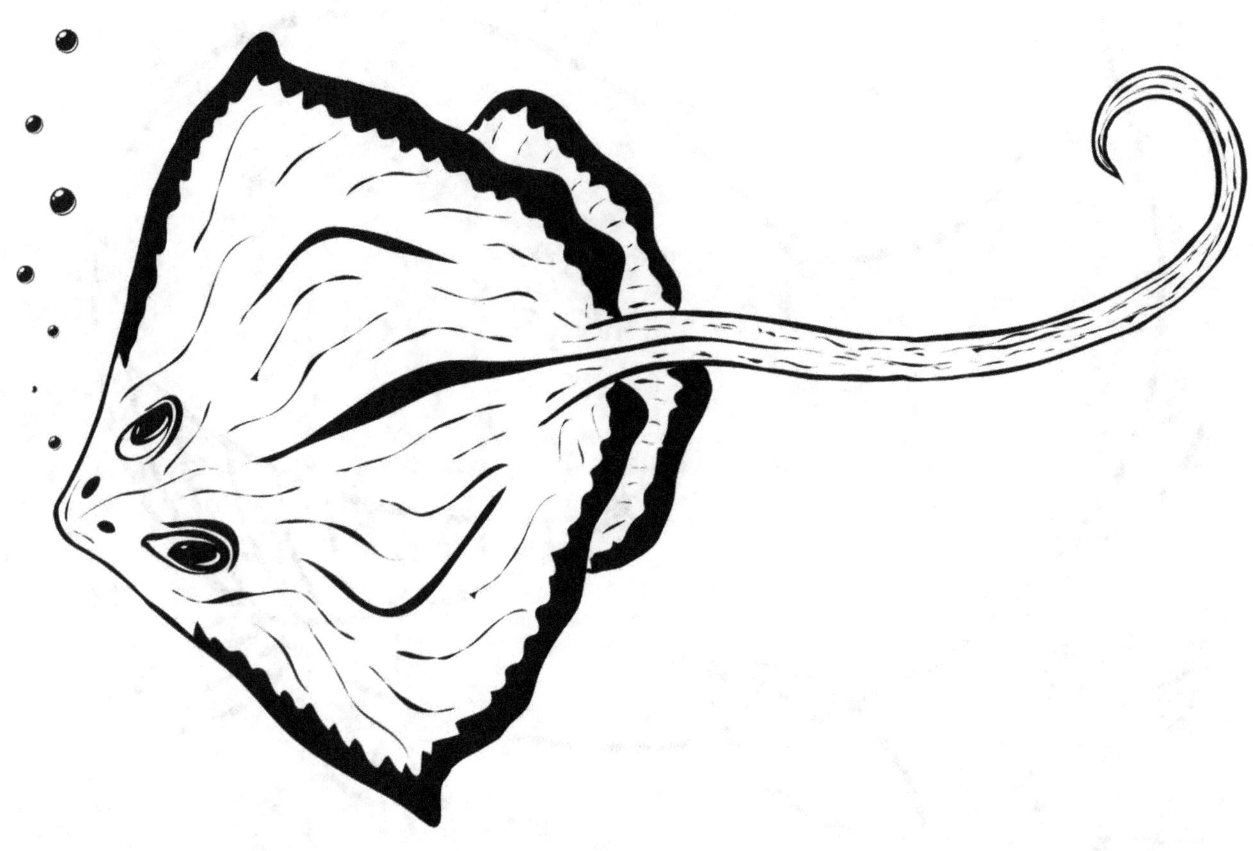

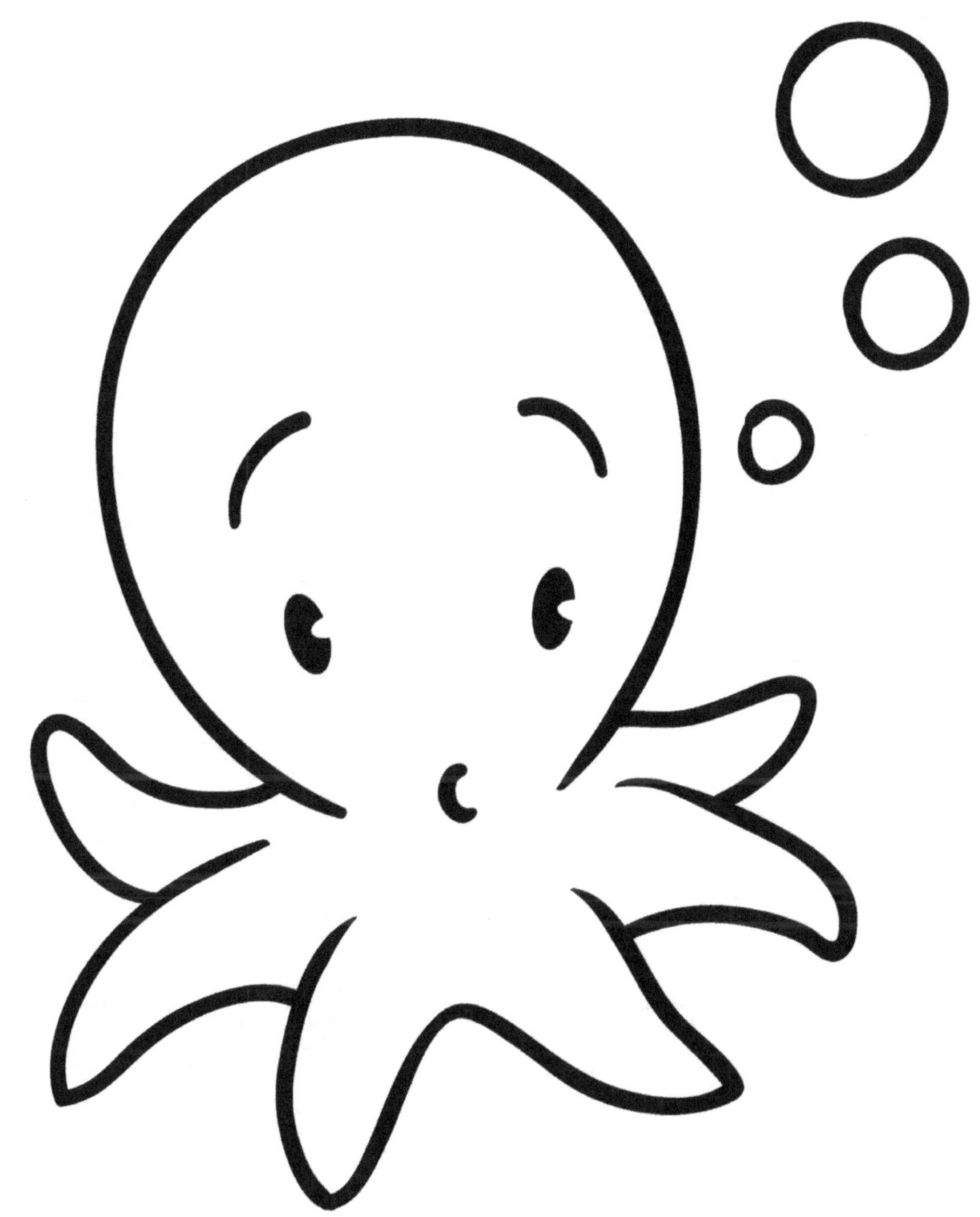

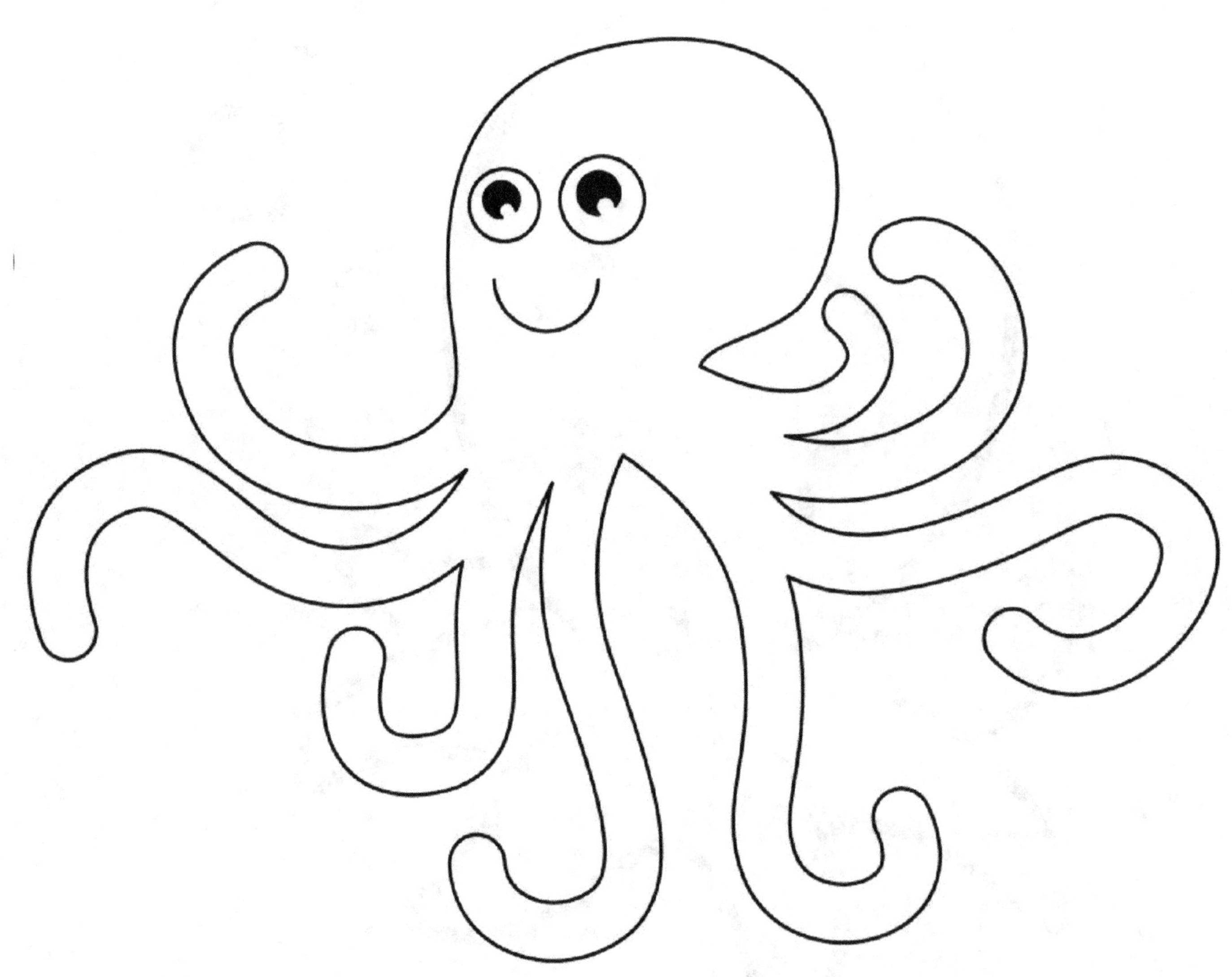

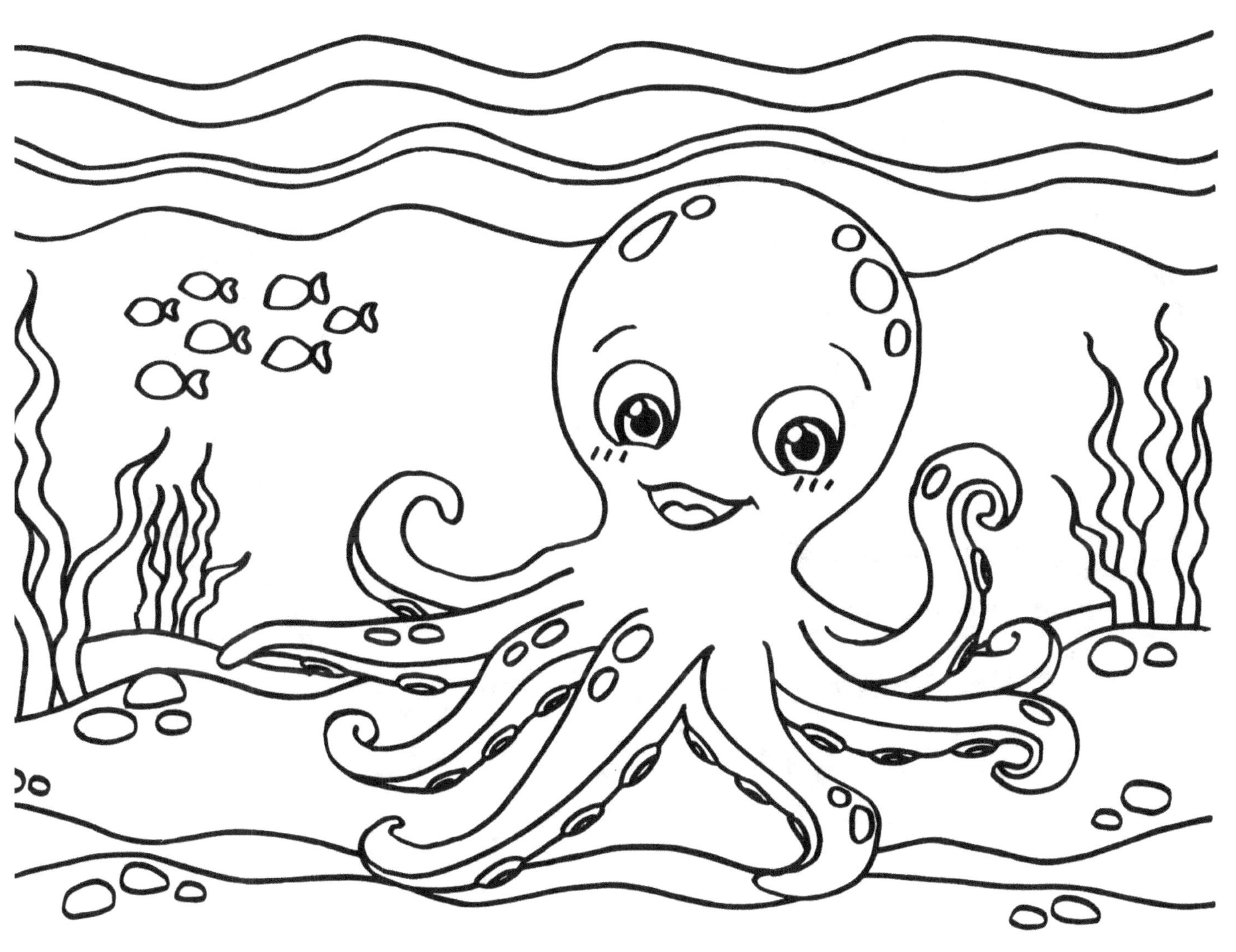

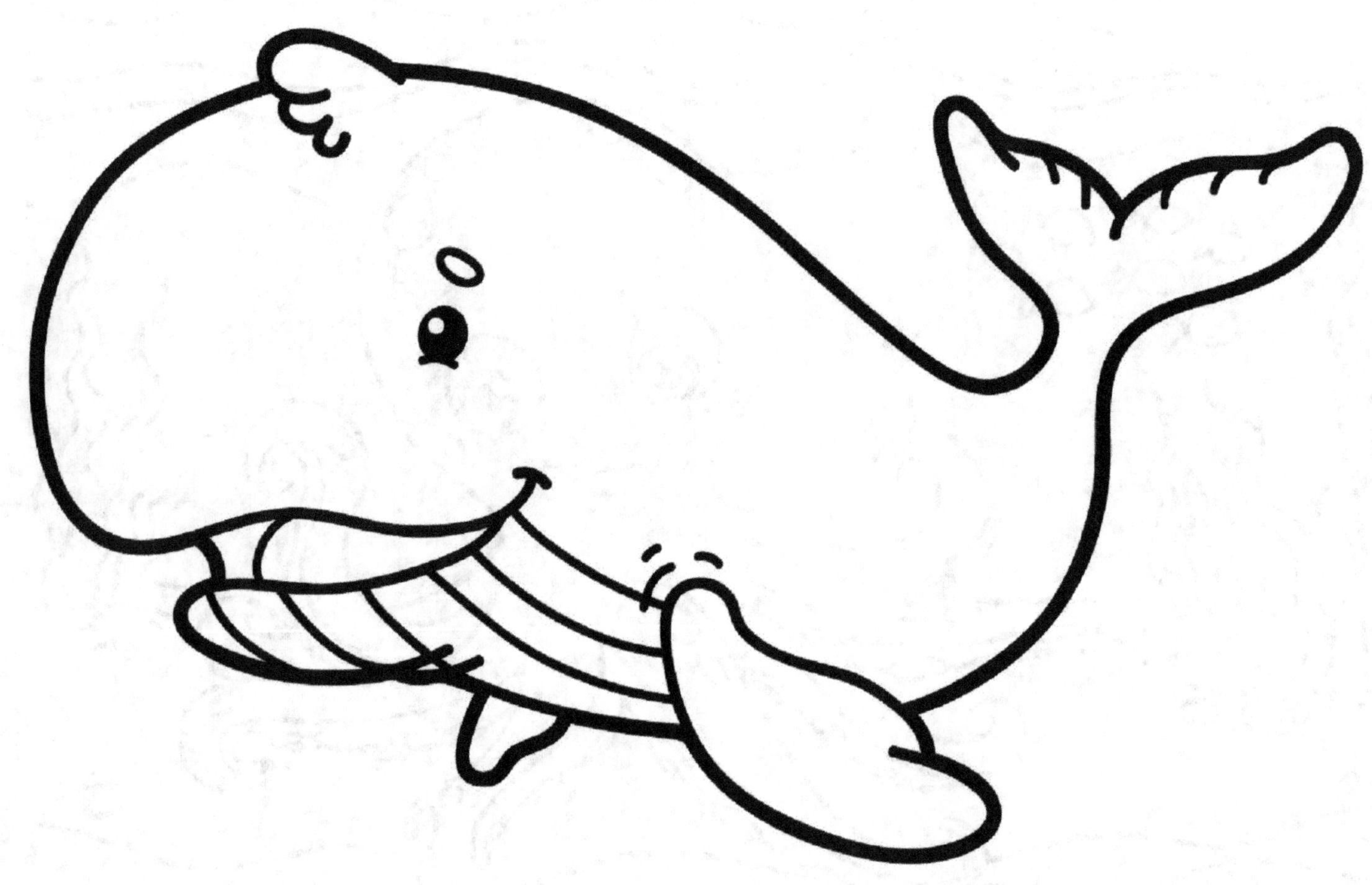

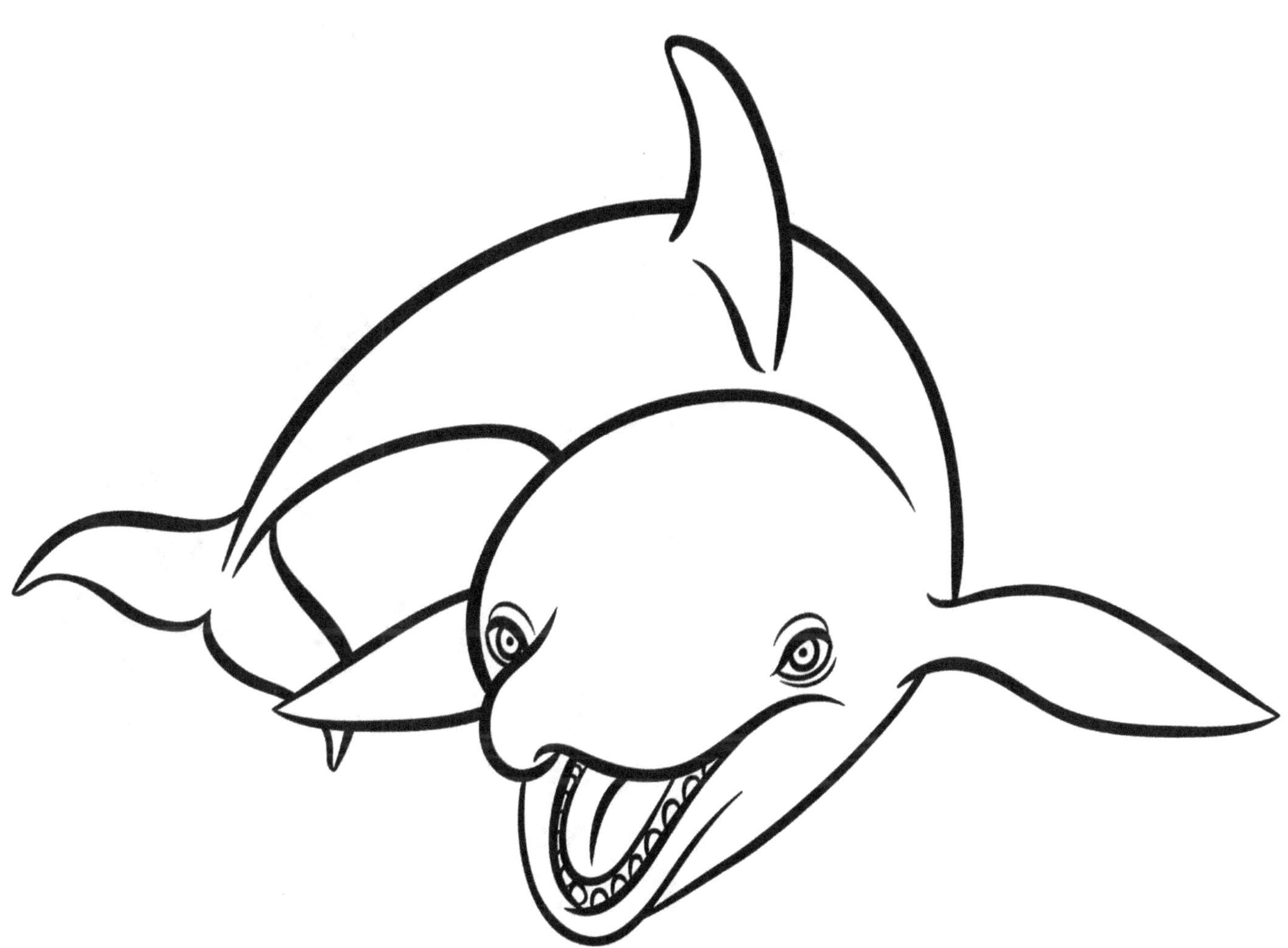

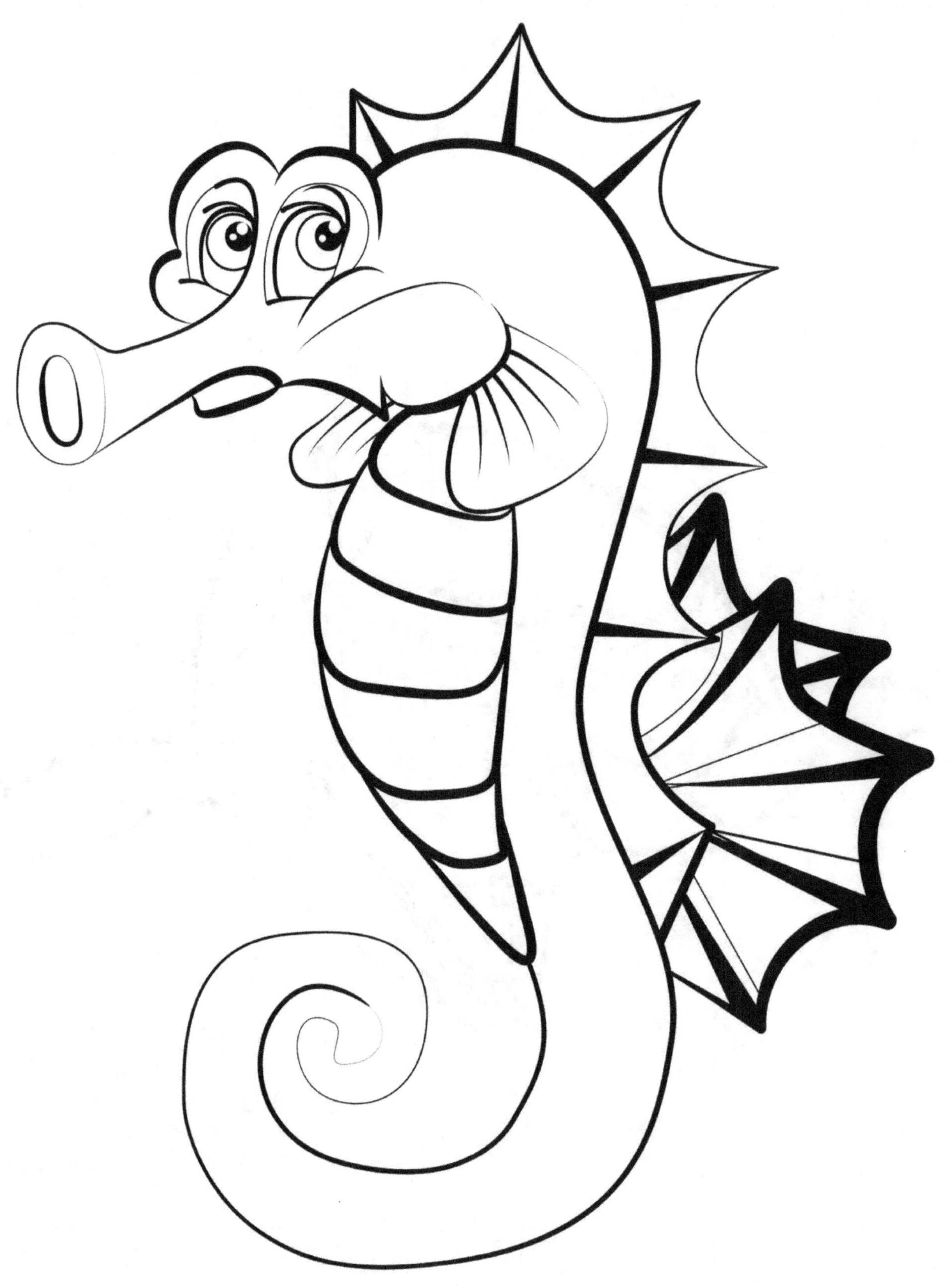

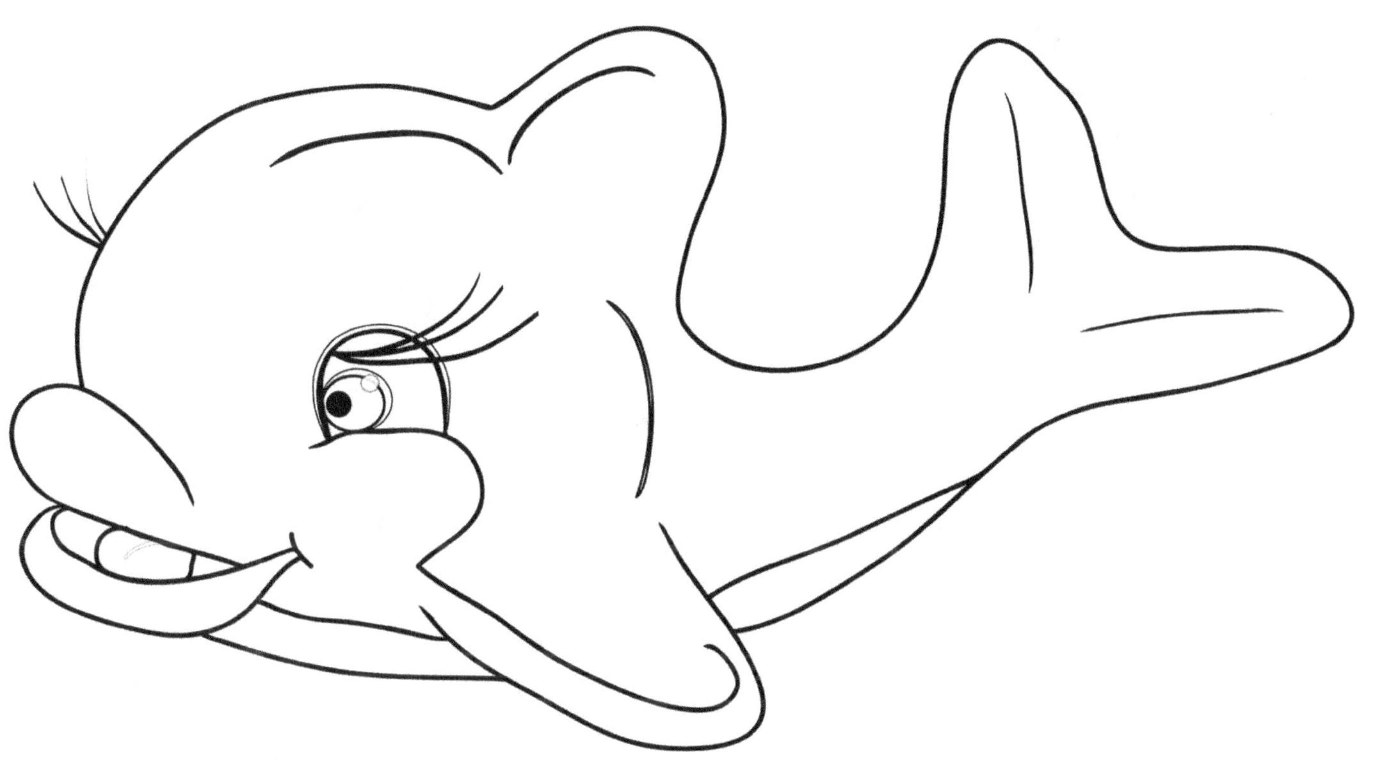

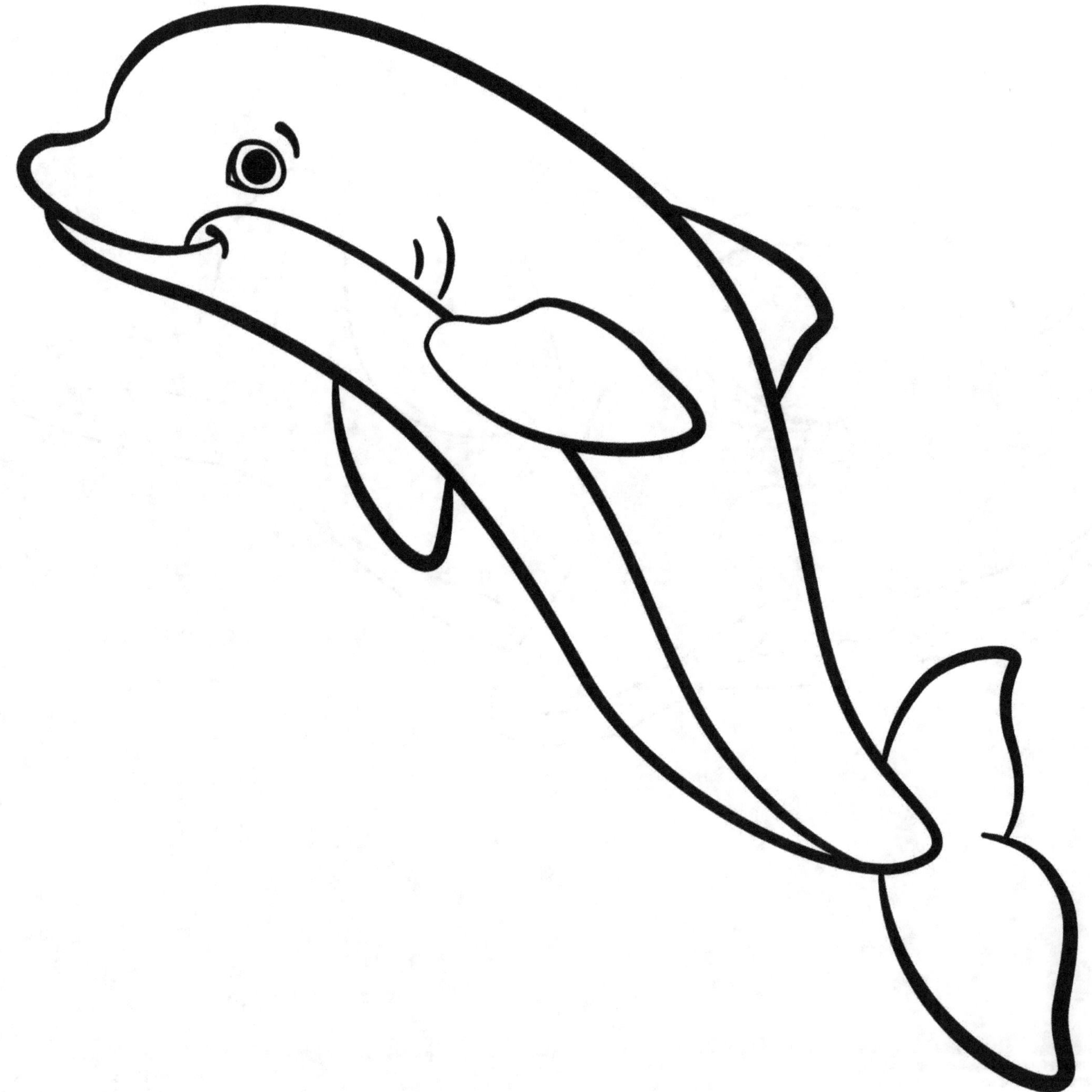

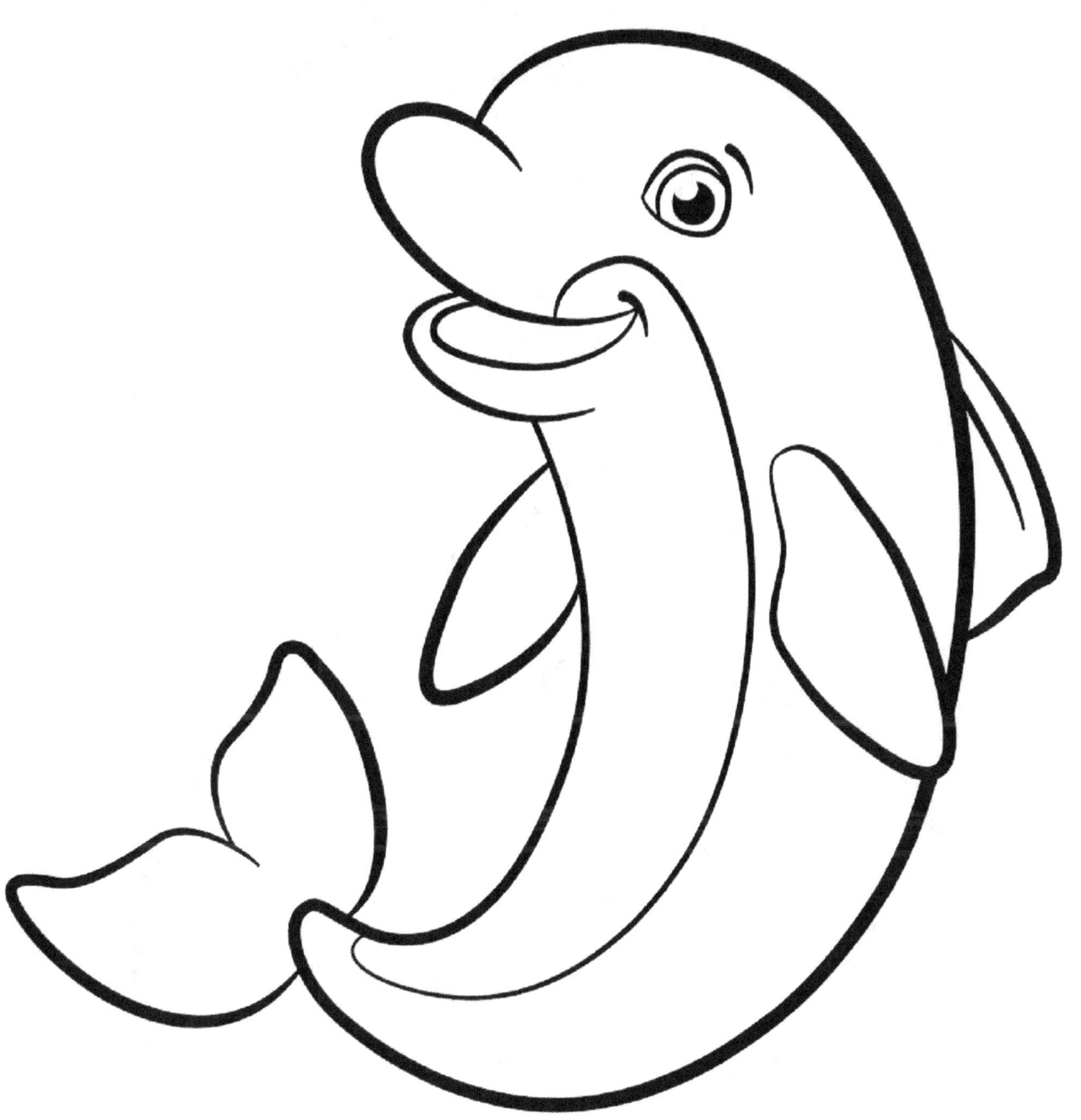

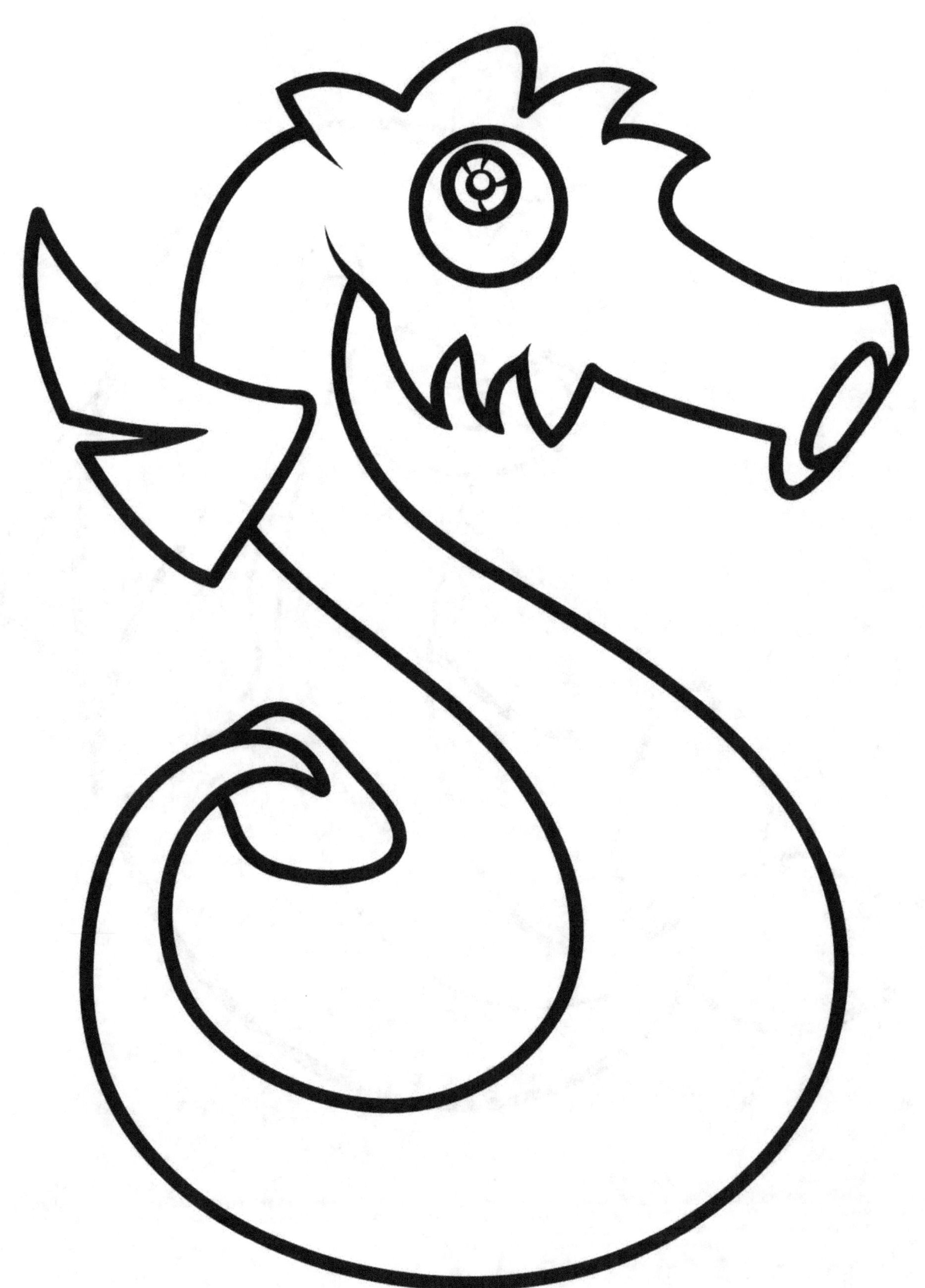

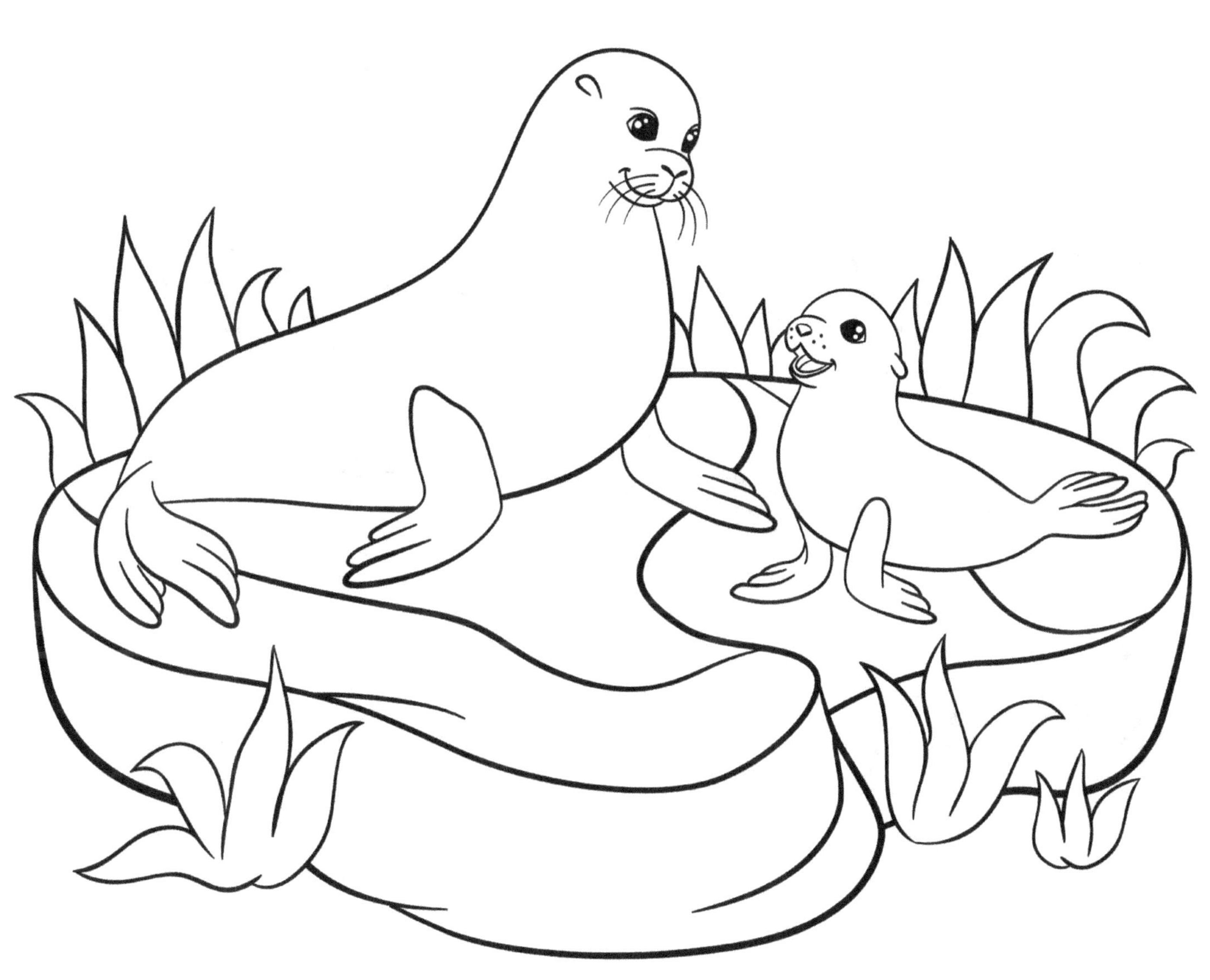

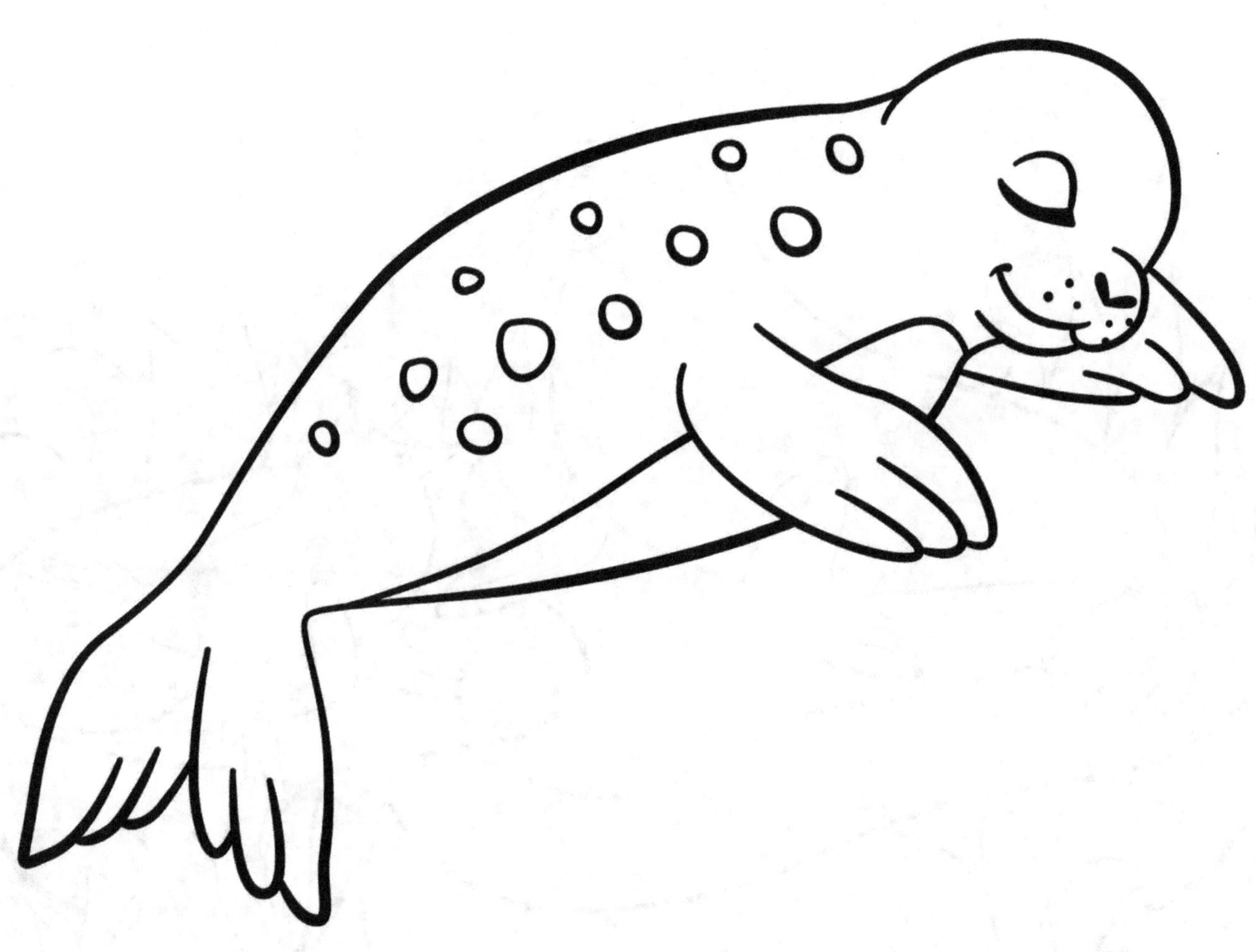

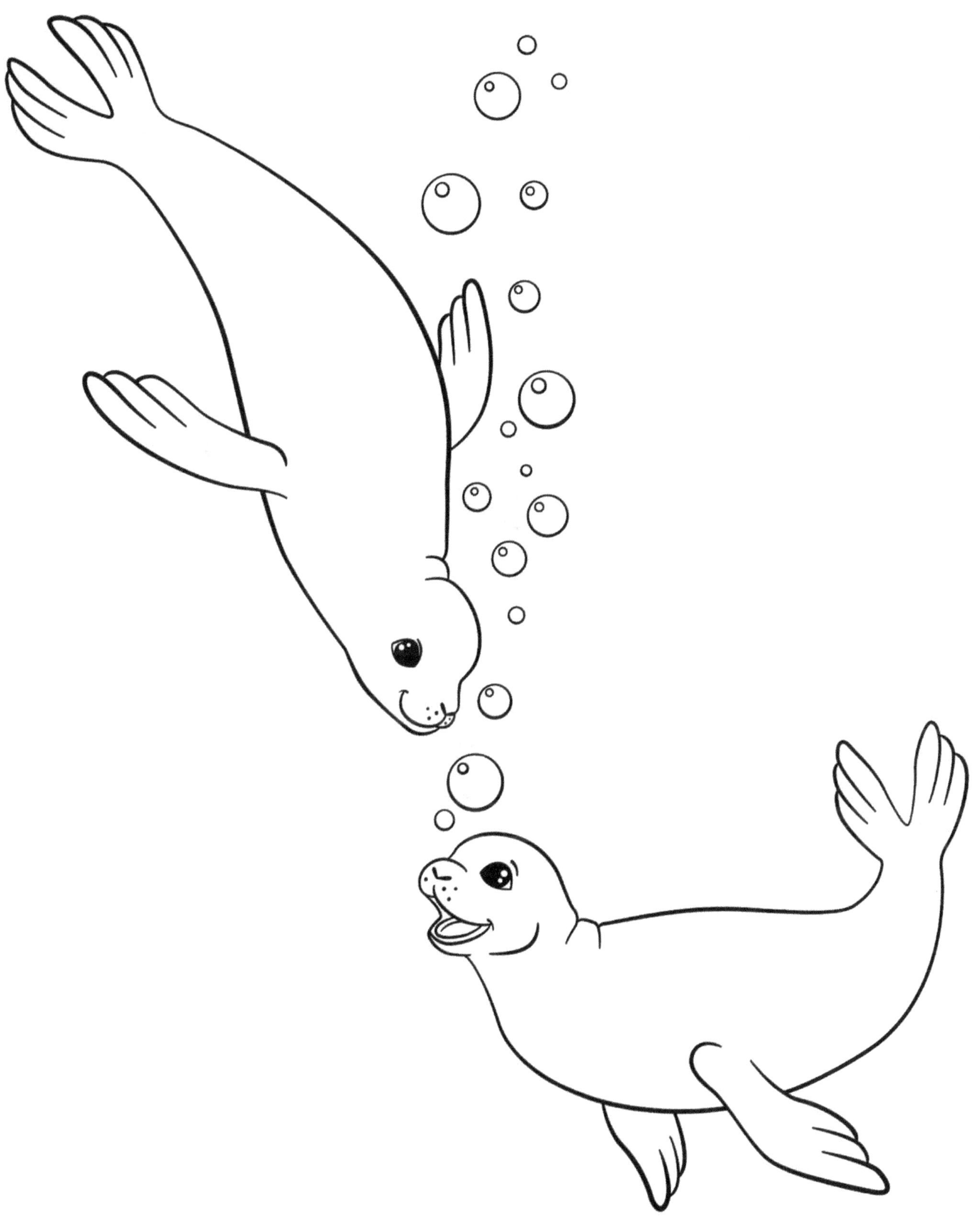

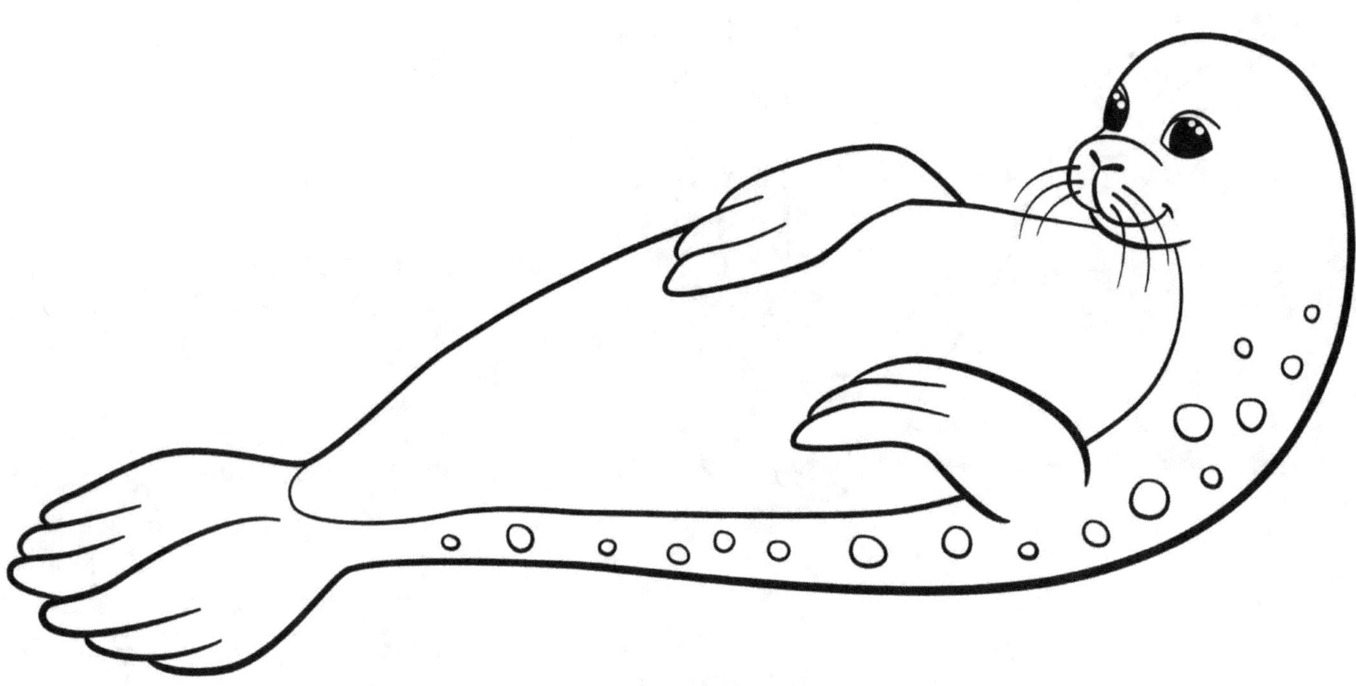

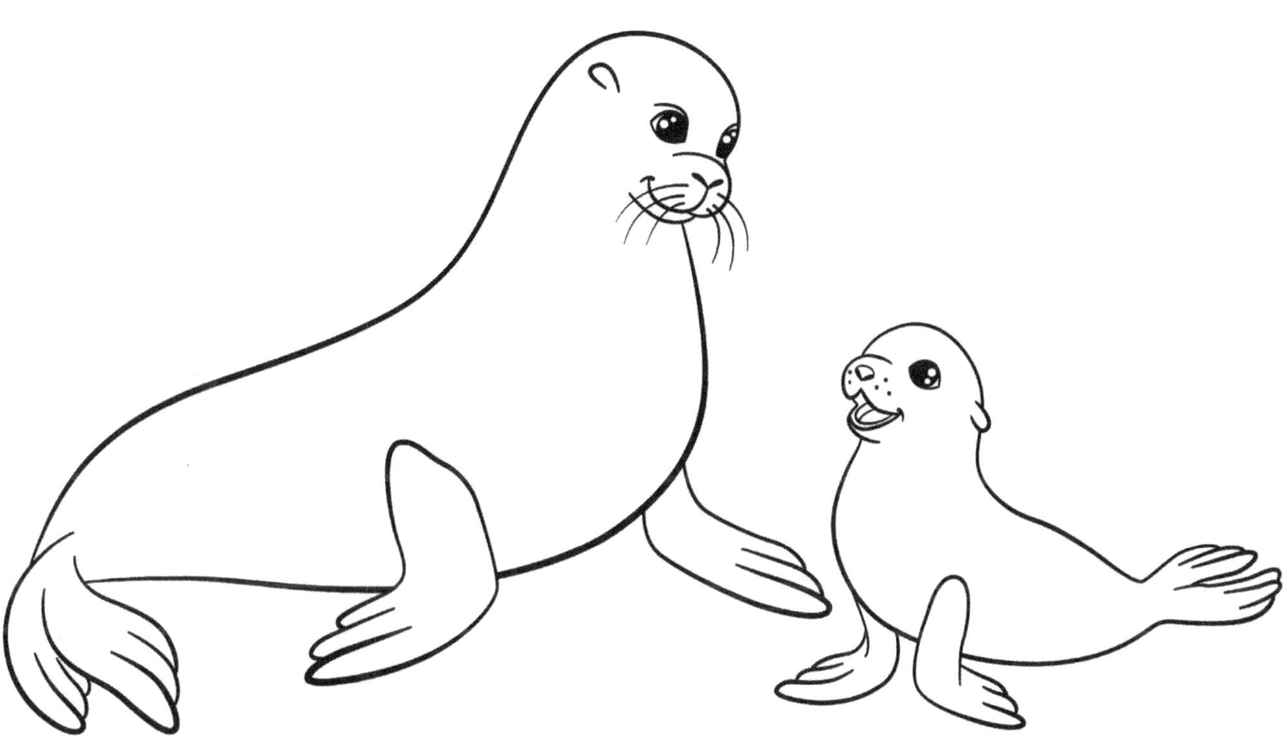

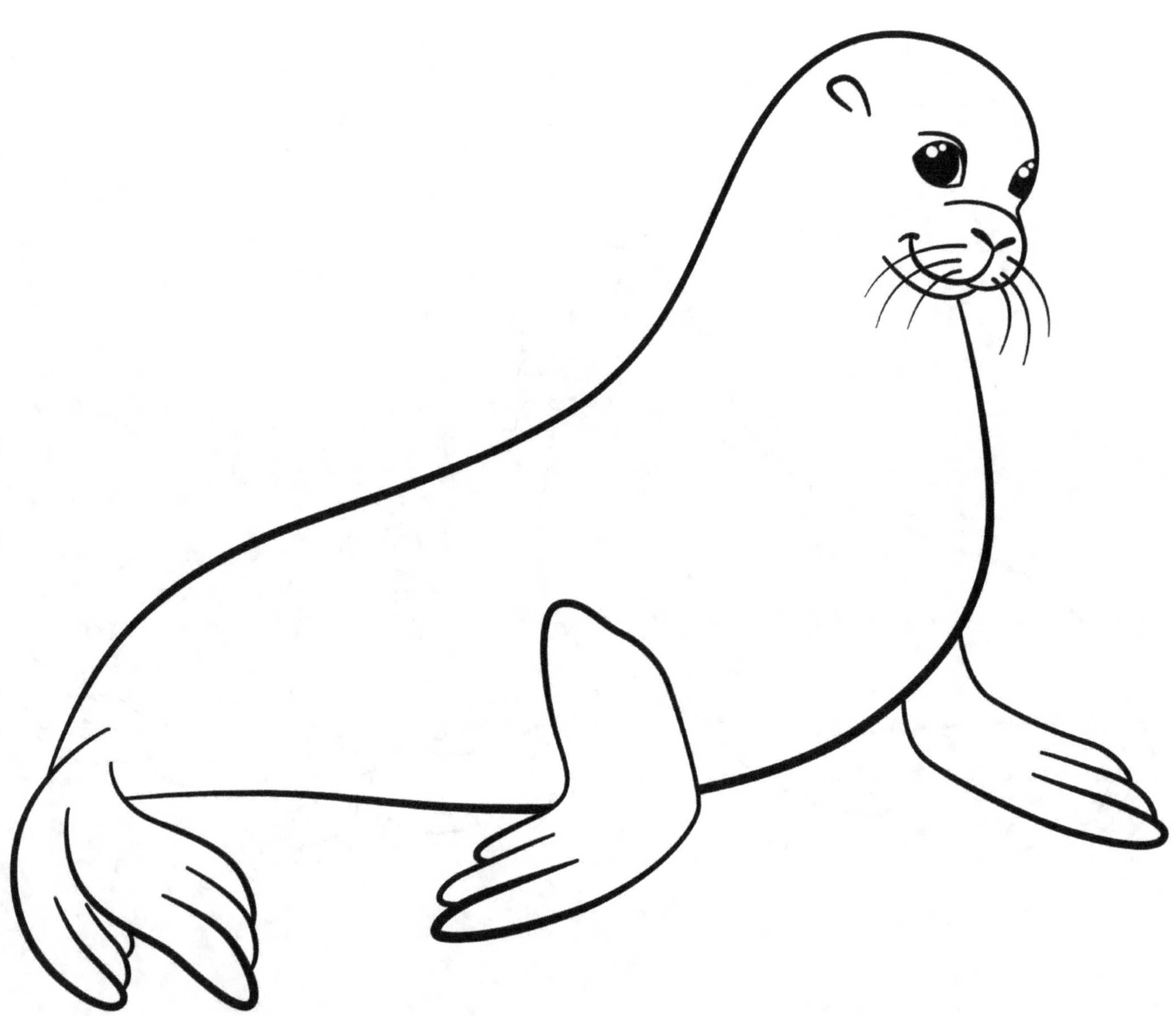

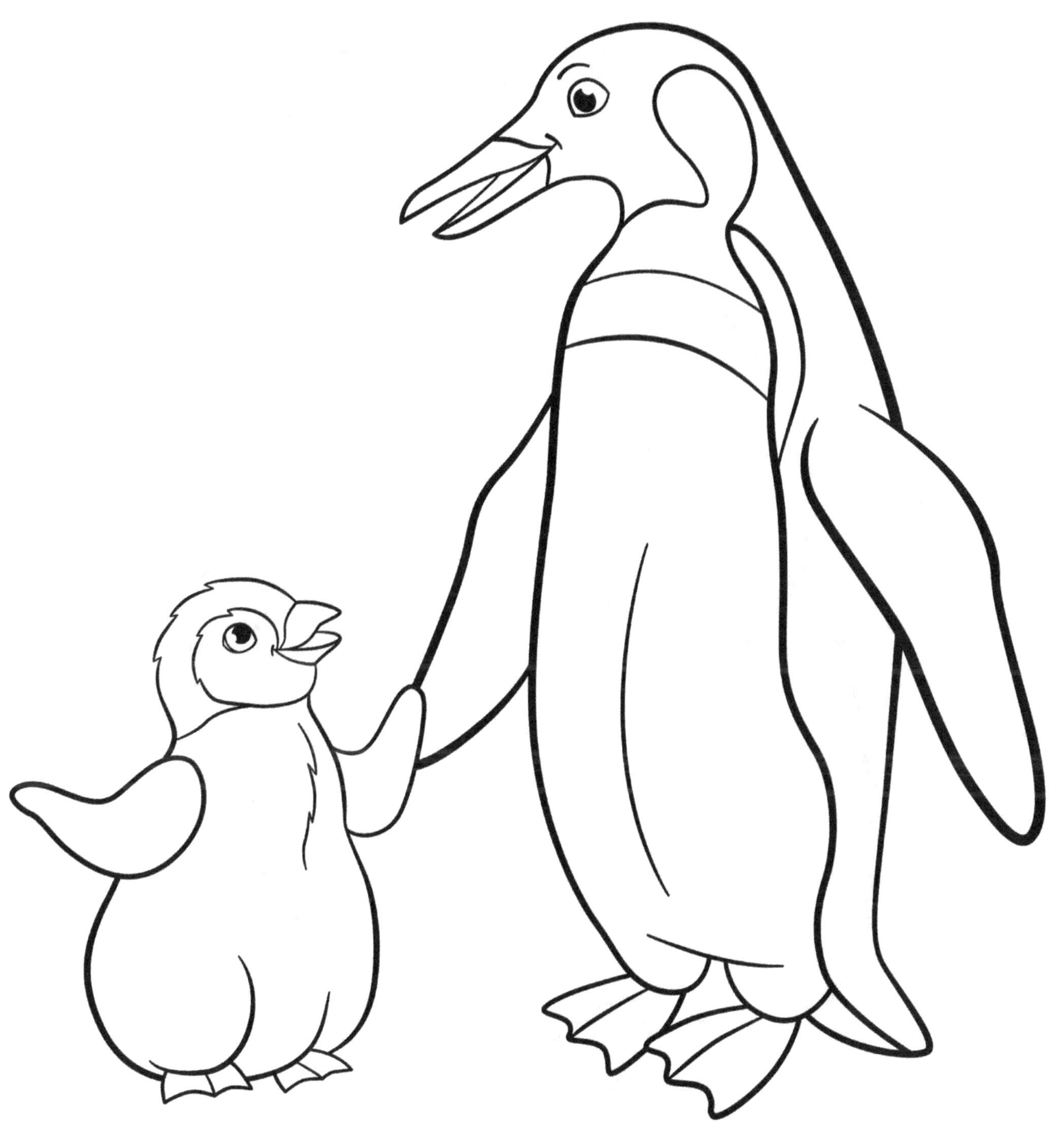

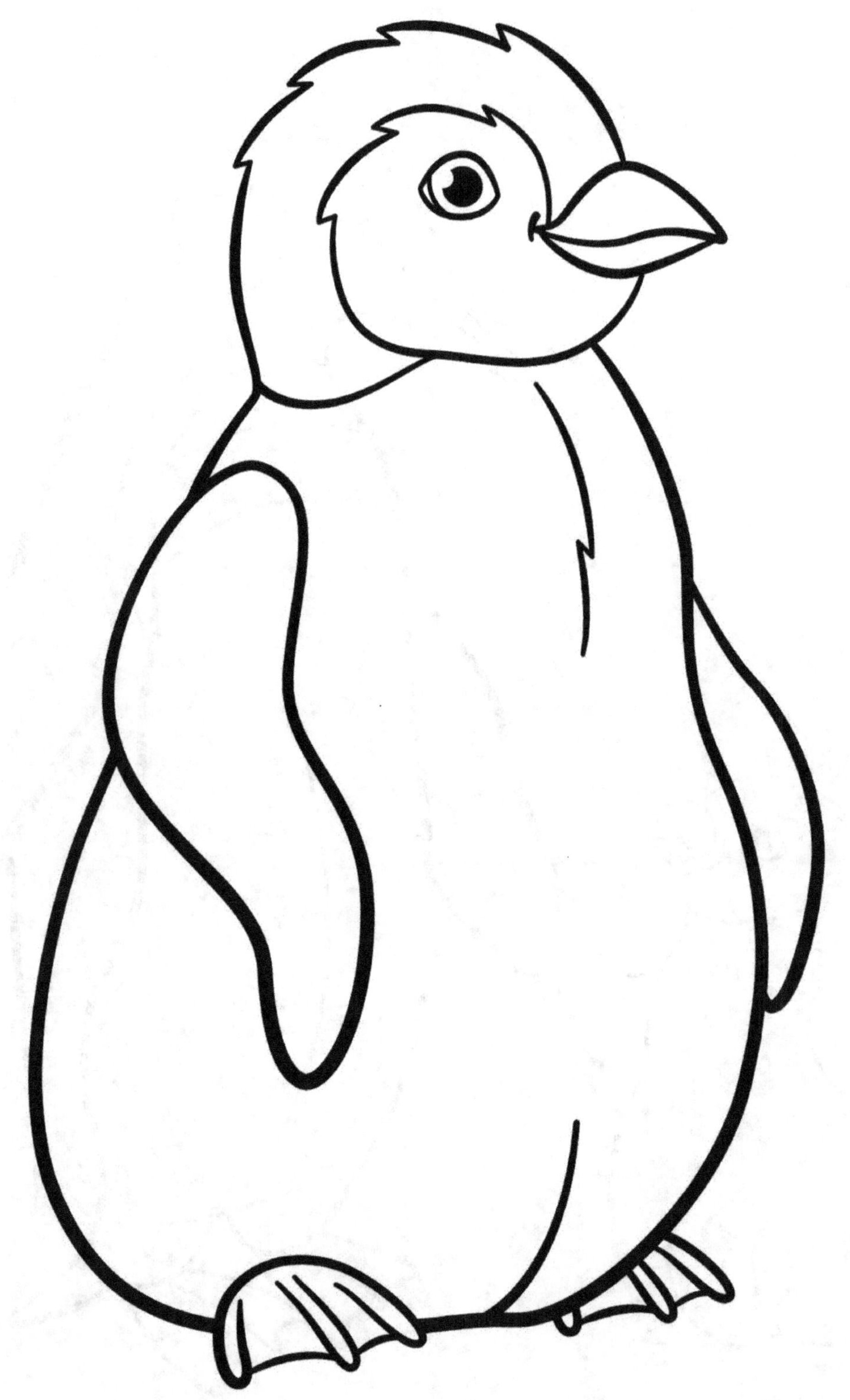

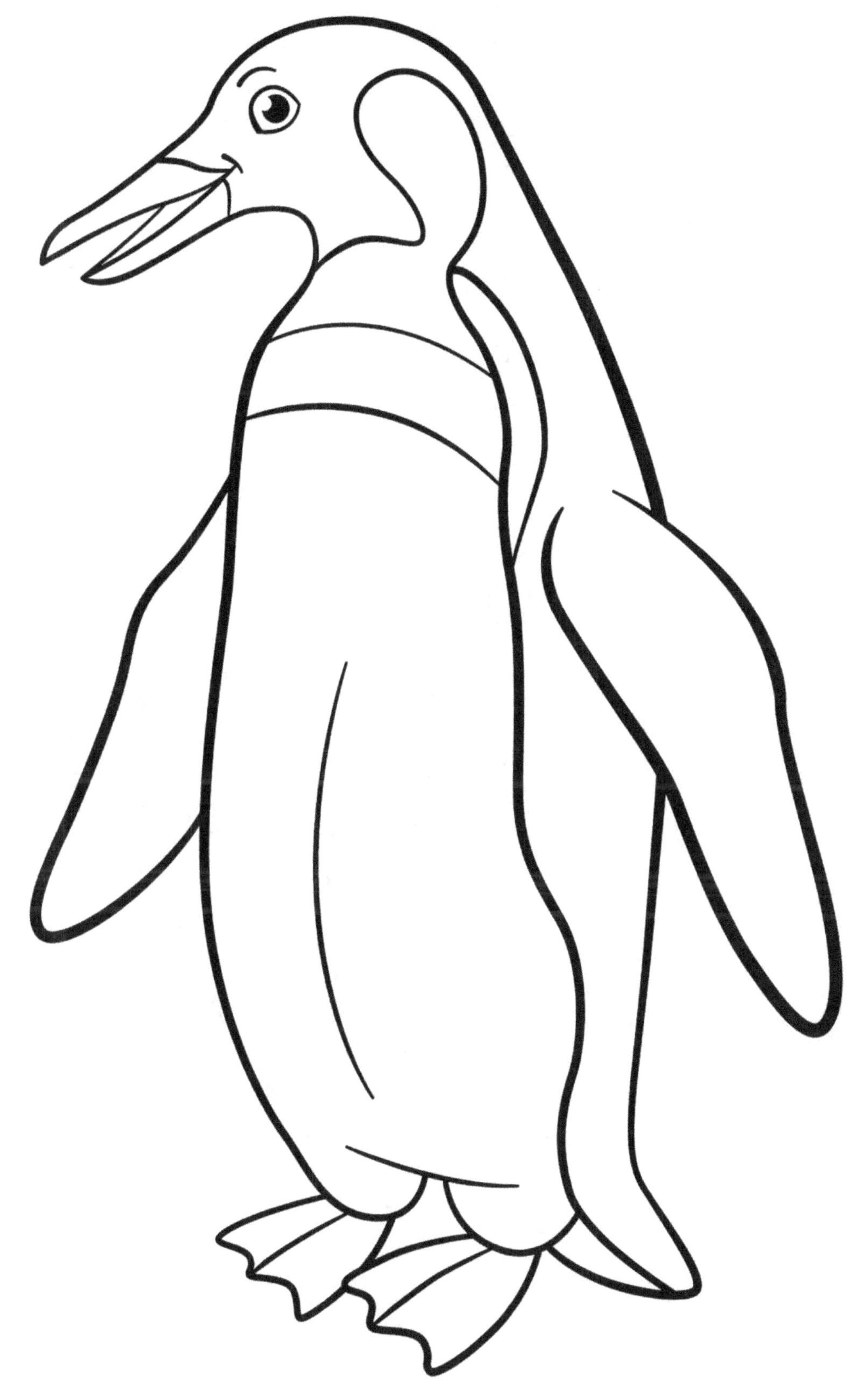

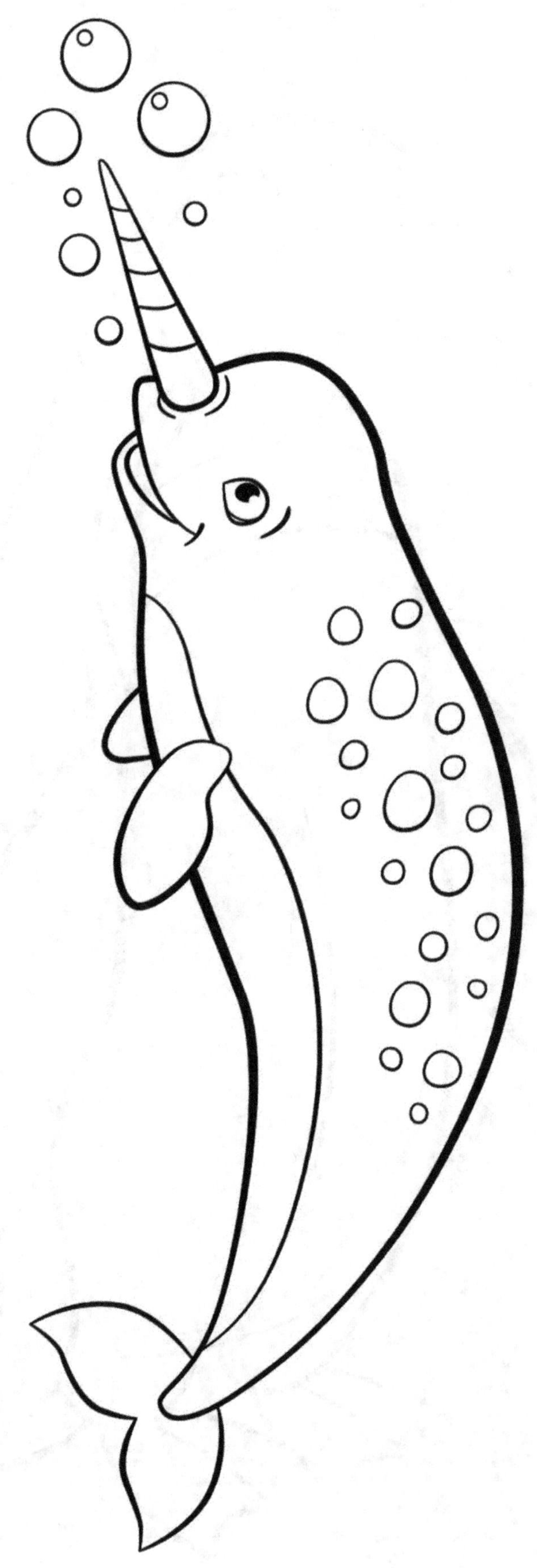

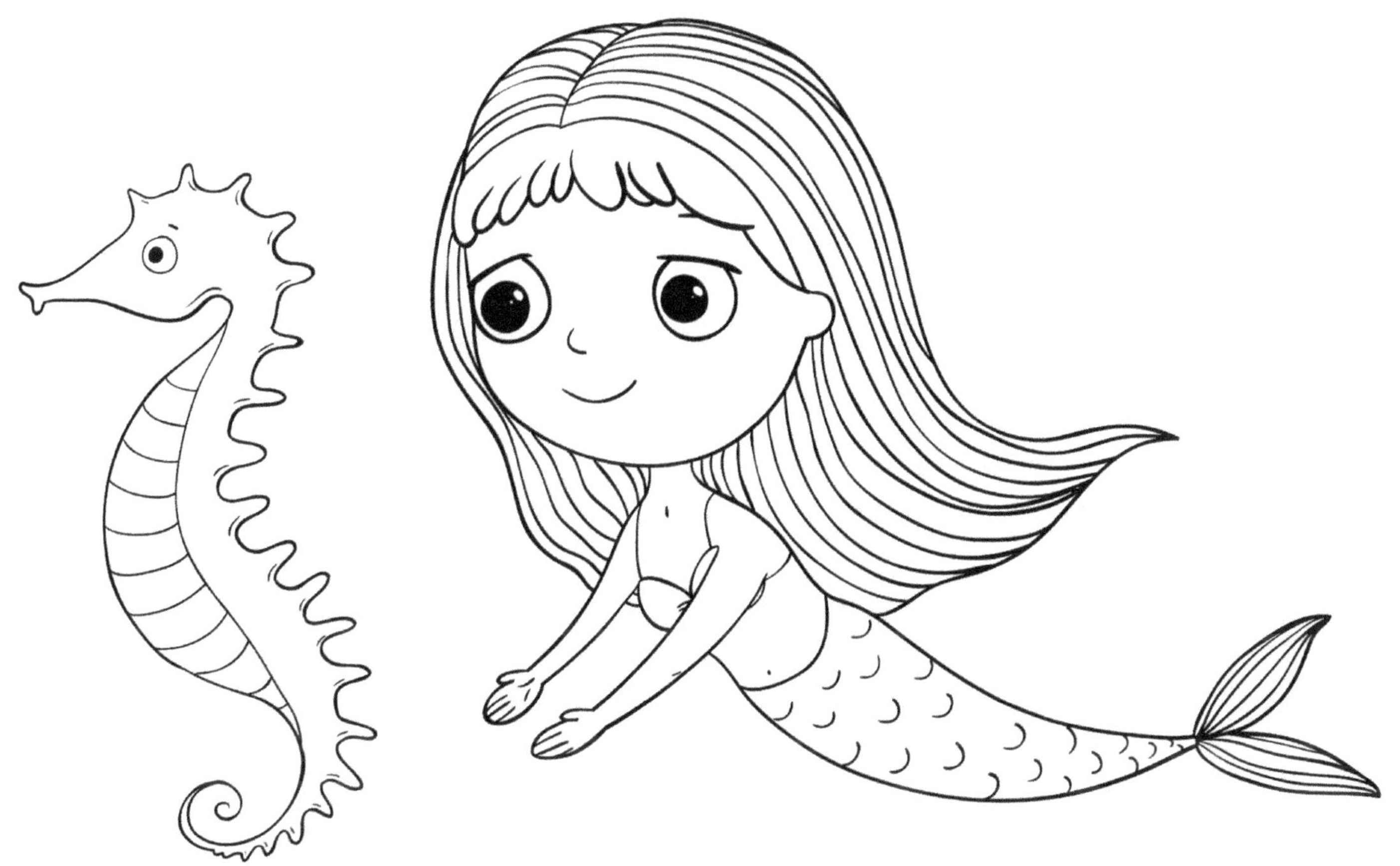